BECOMING AN INDUSTRIALIZED NATION

BECOMING AN INDUSTRIALIZED NATION

ROC's Development on Taiwan

Yuan-li Wu

Published under the Auspices of
The Contemporary U.S.–Asia Research Institute, Inc.
New York, N.Y.

PRAEGER SPECIAL STUDIES • PRAEGER SCIENTIFIC

New York • Philadelphia • Eastbourne, UK
Toronto • Hong Kong • Tokyo • Sydney

Library of Congress Cataloging in Publication Data

Wu, Yuan-li.
  Becoming an industrialized nation.

  "Published under the auspices of the Contemporary
U.S.-Asia Research Institute, Inc., New York, N.Y."
  Includes bibliographies and index.
  1. Taiwan—Economic policy—1945-   . 2. Taiwan—
Industries—1945-   . I. Contemporary U.S.-Asia
Research Institute (New York, N.Y.) II. Title.
HC430.5.Y844 1985   338.951′249   85-9413
ISBN 0-03-004588-6 (alk. paper)

HC
430.5
.W85
1985

Published in 1985 by Praeger Publishers
CBS Educational and Professional Publishing, a Division of CBS Inc.
521 Fifth Avenue, New York, NY 10175 USA

© 1985 by Yuan-li Wu

All rights reserved

56789 052 98765432

Printed in the United States of America on acid-free paper

INTERNATIONAL OFFICES

Orders from outside the United States should be sent to the appropriate address listed below. Orders from areas not listed below should be placed through CBS International Publishing, 383 Madison Ave., New York, NY 10175 USA

Australia, New Zealand
Holt Saunders, Pty. Ltd., 9 Waltham St., Artarmon, N.S.W. 2064, Sydney, Australia

Canada
Holt, Rinehart & Winston of Canada, 55 Horner Ave., Toronto, Ontario, Canada M8Z 4X6

Europe, the Middle East, & Africa
Holt Saunders, Ltd., 1 St. Anne's Road, Eastbourne, East Sussex, England BN21 3UN

Japan
Holt Saunders, Ltd., Ichibancho Central Building, 22-1 Ichibancho, 3rd Floor, Chiyodaku, Tokyo, Japan

Hong Kong, Southeast Asia
Holt Saunders Asia, Ltd., 10 Fl. Intercontinental Plaza, 94 Granville Road, Tsim Sha Tsui East, Kowloon, Hong Kong

Manuscript submissions should be sent to the Editorial Director, Praeger Publishers, 521 Fifth Avenue, New York, NY 10175 USA

IN MEMORY OF MY FATHER
ON THE CENTENNIAL OF HIS BIRTH (1884)

PREFACE

How does a small nation short on natural resources manage to develop at a rapid rate economically? By implementing an externally oriented economic policy making full use of its inexpensive labor would be a highly simplified answer. But how does such a nation continue its high rate of economic development when its labor force is in general no longer so inexpensive, as indeed it should not be if labor has shared amply in the benefits of past development? How should the problem be approached? What are the relevant issues, the obstacles to overcome, and the comparative advantages to be exploited? How do the country's policy makers and the active members of the private sector see the situation for themselves? This book is devoted to a discussion of these points with reference to the island economy of Taiwan and the strategy of continuing development which the authorities of the Republic of China government have shaped in increasing detail for that country.

This is a book, therefore, that looks forward to the future, to the challenges that some other "newly industrializing economies" of today should actually be eager to face in a not too distant future. As we shall find through the discussion, even countries with ample natural resources can derive lessons of value from the Taiwan experience.

This book has become a reality thanks to four contributing factors. Julius Y. Lu, a former student at the University of San Francisco, has been instrumental in gathering and processing a great deal of documentary data for my use. Many academic economists, businessmen, bankers, and ROC officials in the economic field in Taiwan have been most generous with their time and thoughtful comments during repeated interviews and informal discussions in the winters of 1982–83 and 1983–84. The Pacific Cultural Foundation has made it possible for me to visit Taiwan for these interviews and on the spot research. The Hoover Institution has provided me with its continuing and unstinting research support. This study would not have been possible without their assistance.

Since some of the public figures outside the academic circle who have been so helpful to me may prefer to preserve their anonymity, I shall refrain from making individual acknowledgments at this time and place. Among my academic colleagues, however, I wish to acknowledge especially the ideas of Professors Sun Chen, S. C. Tsiang, and Wang Tso-yung whose views on the Taiwan economy have been singularly insightful and enlightening to me.

Last but not least, all my thanks are due to Ms. Thanh Van at Hoover, whose tireless assistance has been a constant reminder of what real work ethic means and how much harder I should be working and to Mrs. Mia Ruhm who kept the several drafts going simultaneously and at a good pace.

Needless to say, by its very nature this book does not offer a precise forecast, still less a prediction of the future growth rate of the Taiwan economy. The impact of greater internationalization, changes in technology, and adjustments of institutions and human behavior are not exactly quantifiable. At the same time, these subjects, which are the focus of discussion in the present volume, are also full of pitfalls for the unwary. Hence the reader is bound to encounter many inadequacies, omissions and downright mistakes, all of which are mine.

Yuan-li Wu
Menlo Park, California
August 1984.

CONTENTS

PREFACE v

1 PROSPECTS OF FUTURE ECONOMIC
  DEVELOPMENT IN THE ROC 1

   Changes in the External Environment of Economic
       Growth 3
    Imperatives in the Domestic Environment 6
      Ideological Goals and Political Imperatives 6
      Economic and Price Stability 7
      Reaching a Plateau 8
    Prospects for Further Growth 13
      Greater Internationalization of the Economy 16
      Coordination of Development, R&D, Education,
       and Manpower Policies 17
      Mobilization of Resources for Growth and
       Structural Change 17
      Enhancement of the Quality of Life and the
       Continued Improvement of Distributive Equity 19
    Notes 19

2 AN EVOLVING ECONOMIC STRATEGY AND
  CONSENSUS 22

    Economic Goals and Policy Emphasis before 1979 23
    Increasing Emphasis on Science and Technology (S&T) 25
    A Policy of Reinvigorated Growth and Internationalization 26
    Issues in Implementation 28
    Streamlining the Fiscal Administration and Financial
      Institutions 30
    The Public-Private Sector Dialogue 31
    The Interest Rate, Money Supply, and Equity-Debt
      Ratio—A Tripartite Debate 33
    The 1982 Consensus among Economists 34
    A Fundamental Real Consensus 36
    Notes 37

Chapter		Page
3	**INWARD TRANSFER AND INTERNAL GROWTH OF KNOWLEDGE-INTENSIVE INDUSTRIES**	39
	Introduction	39
	Increasing the Profitability of New Investment	41
	Embodied Knowledge and the Human Resource	42
	Industry and R&D Priorities	45
	A Recapitulation of the 1983 Government Program to Promote Science and Technology	47
	A Preliminary Review of the Record	48
	Examples from Agricultural R&D	49
	Introducing the Time Dimension	51
	Increasing Production and Value-Added	51
	Notes	51
4	**INSTITUTIONAL DEVELOPMENT AND THE MOBILIZATION OF CAPITAL**	53
	A Dual Task in Channeling Savings to Investment	53
	Characteristics of Taiwan's Financial Markets and Business Behavior	54
	A Question of Equal Access to the Capital Market	59
	Improving the Allocation and Use of Savings	61
	Financing of High Tech and Other Growth Industries	63
	Reforming the Securities Market	64
	Risk-taking and Venture Capital Investment	67
	Notes	68
5	**MEETING THE DEMAND FOR SCIENTIFIC AND TECHNICAL MANPOWER (S&T)**	70
	Economic Development from the Perspective of Interindustry Transfers of Labor	70
	Taiwan's Development Needs and Supply of Specialized Manpower	71
	Economic Growth and its Educational Infrastructure	74
	Vocational Training and Higher Education	74
	Educational Expenditure and Development Policy	78

Chapter	Page
Institutional Coordination and Adjustment in Manpower Planning	80
Foreign Business Participation in Training Technical Workers	83
Unresolved Issues	83
Notes	84

6 LIBERALIZATION OF THE EXTERNAL ECONOMY AND INTERNATIONALIZATION 86

Broadening of External Economic Relations	86
Export Expansion and Structural Change	88
Diversification of Export Markets	91
Liberalization and Changes in the Trading System	97
Bilateral U.S.-ROC Trade Negotiations in 1978	97
Customs Simplifications and Tariff Reductions	98
Customs Duties as a Source of Revenue	99
Lowering Licensing Controls and Direct Government Intervention	100
Relaxation of Exchange Control	102
Travel	103
Labor Income	103
Investment Income	103
Private Remittances	104
Developing an International Financial Network	106
The Taiwan (ROC) Fund	106
A Venture Capital Fund	106
An Offshore Financial Center	107
Other Institutions in the Offing?	107
The Expanded Concept of a Regional Trade Center	108
Power Politics and International Economics	110
Notes	111

7 BEHAVIORAL ACCOMMODATION TO ECONOMIC DEVELOPMENT: PROBING CULTURAL ROOTS 114

Motives and Attitudes Underlying Taiwan's Economic Development	114

xi

Chapter	Page
Is Thriftiness Inborn?	114
Dedication to Education and the Drive for Self-Improvement	116
From Strong Competitiveness to Unfair Competition	117
Paying for External Costs and Taking a "Free Ride"	119
Dependency on the Government?	121
Economic Development and the Confucian Ethic	122
From Confucian Self-Cultivation to Social Responsibility	123
Internalizing Sanctions as a Complement to the Rule of Law	125
Knowledge and Reason Underlying Economic Progress and Freedom	125
Attitudinal Change and Extending the Planning Horizon	126
A Postscript	127
Notes	129
INDEX	133
ABOUT THE AUTHOR	139

BECOMING AN INDUSTRIALIZED NATION

1

PROSPECTS OF FUTURE ECONOMIC DEVELOPMENT IN THE ROC

As one of the few newly industrializing countries of our time, the economy of the Republic of China on Taiwan has been the subject of a number of studies during the last decade. In its 1979 World Development Report, the World Bank included the ROC in a select list of four East Asian nations that had "achieved remarkably fast GDP growth and virtually eliminated absolute poverty."[1] Table 1.1 below presents for these four economies GNP per capita in 1981, the annual growth rate of real GDP in 1970-81, and the foreign debt service ratio in comparison with the corresponding data for the United States, Japan, the PRC, and the World Bank's "upper middle income" group of countries as a whole. Taiwan stands out very favorably in this comparison. Since the period covered included the first and second major oil price hikes initiated by OPEC in the 1970s, this record was all the more impressive for economies totally dependent upon imported oil. To the World Bank in 1979 there were "insights into the process of structural transformation" which these "middle income," "semi-industrialized" countries can offer other later comers. This volume is written for the same purpose but will focus on one aspect of the Taiwan economy, namely, its prospects for continuing growth and the lesson its strategy and performance will have for less developed countries (LDCs) and middle income nations elsewhere.

TABLE 1.1. Comparative Indicators of Economic Performance

		GNP per Capita (in U.S. dollars) 1981	Average Annual Growth Rate of Real GDP (in percent) 1970-81	Debt Services (percent of export of goods and services) 1981
The four NICs	Korea	1,700	9.1	13.1
	Taiwan	2,563	10.1	4.7
	Hong Kong	5,100	9.9	...
	Singapore	5,240	8.5	0.8
Upper middle income group	High	5,670 (Trinidad & Tobago)	10.1 (Taiwan)	31.9 (Brazil)
	Average or or Median	2,490[W]	5.6[W]	15.4[W]
	Low	1,700 (Korea)	1.9[a] (Argentina)	0.8 (Singapore)
Other comparisons	PRC	300	5.5	...
	USA	12,820	2.9	n.a.
	Japan	10,080	4.5	n.a.
	Industrial market economies	11,120[W]	3.0[W]	n.a.

[a] The negative average growth rate of 5.4 percent for Lebanon has been disregarded in identifying the lowest growth rate for 1980-81.

[W] Denotes "weighted."

Throughout this volume, " . . . " indicates no information.

All currency values expressed in "New Taiwan Dollars" bear the sign "NT$"; all other $ signs, whether specifically so described or not, express values in United States dollars.

Source: For all the above countries except Taiwan, World Bank, *World Development Report 1983* (New York: Oxford University Press, 1983), Table 1, pp. 148-151 and 178-179. For Taiwan, *Taiwan Statistical Data Book, 1983* and *Statistical Yearbook of the Republic of China, 1983*, compiled by the Council for Economic Planning and Development (EDP). (The Bank no longer publishes data on Taiwan since the PRC became a Bank member in 1980.)

CHANGES IN THE EXTERNAL ENVIRONMENT OF ECONOMIC GROWTH

The ROC economy on Taiwan registered a remarkably steady and high growth record during the two decades between the Korean truce (1953) and the armistice in Vietnam (1973). An important facet of this growth was its acceleration starting from the mid-1960s when U.S. economic aid to Taiwan ended. Real GNP growth gathered speed through 1973 when the exceedingly sharp price increases demanded by the oil cartel towards the end of the year ushered in a prolonged period of worldwide economic adjustment to the resultant inflation and reduced economic activity, the effect of which affected Taiwan severely. The acceleration of Taiwan's economic expansion without foreign aid, however, extended well beyond 1971 when the communist People's Republic of China took over the ROC's seat in the United Nations. The rising growth path extended even beyond 1972 when Nixon and Chou En-lai put their signatures to the Shanghai communiqué, thus marking another step in the progressive disengagement of the United States from the ROC. The island republic's remarkable economic resilience and political stability against great adversity and the confidence shown by its authorities and business community demonstrated one undeniable fact for the benefit of all developing countries including Taiwan. That is, given the proper domestic environment and incentives and certain external economic conditions, self-sustained economic growth in a stable political environment is entirely possible even in an island economy that is heavily populated, poorly endowed with natural resources (including some, like petroleum, for which there are no adequate substitutes in the short run), and subject to severe hostile international pressures. Planners in other LDCs could well ask: If Taiwan can make it under such conditions, then why not we? For Taiwan the question is: How should we continue? Yet it would be foolhardy to dismiss lightly the adverse impact of certain fundamental political and economic conditions underlying Taiwan's economic development. The adverse events of the 1970s were merely the tip of an iceberg.

First, while the debacle of the precipitate and wholesale withdrawal of U.S. forces from South Vietnam in 1975 and the fall of that country were by no means an inevitable consequence of the 1973 armistice,[2] U.S. willingness, even eagerness, to conclude an armistice, leaving its South Vietnamese ally to face a powerful communist army virtually alone on the ground, departed radically from the pattern set in Korea 20 years earlier. The psychological resources of the American nation that could be brought to bear in 1973-75 were apparently no longer sufficient to maintain security in the region by the United States' own strength. An active search for a more viable formula for U.S. foreign policy was on. Since the Soviet Union was viewed as the chief adversary of the United States, it was only natural that the communist government of mainland China, which for a number of years had become openly estranged from its erstwhile Soviet ally, would be looked upon by some U.S. policy makers, wistfully as it were, as a potential, if not already actual, source of "parallel strategic interest."[3] China had nuclear arms in addition to a numerically very large conventional force; it shared a long border with the Soviet Union; it was populous and possessed large natural resources. To the government on Taiwan all this means that instead of a reliable U.S. ally providing a security screen in the Taiwan Strait, the ROC would henceforth have to cope with the hostility of its communist adversary essentially on its own. Economically, the long-term prospects of the People's Republic becoming a major competitor on the world market also began to loom. The sustained psychological warfare mounted by Peking to isolate Taiwan politically, hoping thereby to weaken the latter's economy indirectly, has added to the latter's sense of military insecurity. Since 1979,[4] this alteration of the external environment has given rise to two newly expanded tasks for Taiwan's economic policy: to devote a greater share of technological and material resources to defense and to provide an enlarged role for the country's foreign economic relations, substituting, wherever possible, international economic presence for conventional diplomatic relations. Of course, these are not really new policy requirements but they have acquired wider public appreciation in Taiwan and a much sharper focus in ROC policy making than heretofore.

A second blow taking aim at Taiwan's international economic standing came in the spring of 1980 when the ROC was ousted from the International Monetary Fund and the World Bank. Although the Taiwan Relations Act (Public Law 96-8, April 10, 1979, 93 Stat. 14) which Congress had passed to preserve and promote "extensive, close, and friendly commercial... relations" with Taiwan, unequivocally stipulated, "Nothing in this Act may be construed as a basis for supporting the exclusion or expulsion of Taiwan from continued membership in any international financial institution or any other international organization" (Section 2, (b) (1)), the United States made no effort to stop the ROC's ouster from the two Bretton Woods institutions. This meant that after May 1980 the resources of both organizations would not have been available to aid Taiwan directly, or indirectly through participation in or guarantee of commercial credit, had such a need arisen. It was only in 1982, when the PRC cast its eye on the Asian Development Bank, that the United States took a different stand and succeeded in side-tracking a Japanese effort to seat Peking at the expense of Taipei. The IMF-World Bank case taught Taiwan another lesson on international political behavior and the importance of maintaining on its own external liquidity and credit worthiness.

In the third place, the repeated oil price hikes (especially initially in 1973-74 and again in 1979) highlighted certain basic economic facts. (1) For an island economy short on natural resources, security of supply, en route and at source, is of paramount importance because of the country's critical dependence on imports. (2) An increasing volume of imports necessitated by the desired continuation of economic growth points to the need for an uninterrupted expansion of foreign exchange earnings from exports and investments in foreign countries. (3) A precondition of increasing investment income from abroad is to build up external capital investments through sustained export surpluses.

A fourth lesson which hit home during the recession in the early 1980s is the vulnerability of such export-dependent economies as Taiwan to developments in the rest of the world, especially in their principal export markets. Unlike countries exporting primary commodities, which often suffer from price instability,[5] Taiwan's exports suffer when demand falls as a result of declining income abroad. Competition in foreign markets on the part of third countries, for example, South Korea, Singapore, and Hong Kong, has sharpened under conditions of declining income. The demand for protection by specific import-competing domestic producers have also increased in the importing countries. Not only do these developments adversely affect Taiwan's earnings, their unfavorable impact on overall employment and economic activity is magnified by the increasingly larger share export demand constitutes in Taiwan's GNP.

IMPERATIVES IN THE DOMESTIC ENVIRONMENT

Since economic development is a continuous process, it must build upon the successes and failures of the past. Moreover, where long-term national goals exist and are taken seriously, as is the case with the ROC, secular objectives of ideological and political origins play an important role in policy making. Yet long-term economic and other objectives cannot be immune to short-term practical demands, and policies for long-run economic growth will from time to time have to accommodate shorter-run cyclical conditions and specific measures designed to alleviate them.

Ideological Goals and Political Imperatives

The government of the Republic of China, under the long-time administration of the Nationalist Party (Kuomintang), traces its basic policy to the doctrines first enunciated by the late Sun Yat-sen, founder of the Party and the Republic that came into existence after the 1911 revolution. Sun's principles of "nationalism, democracy and people's livelihood" are not just the underlying ideas of a political party's platform; they are the leitmotif of the ROC constitution.[6]

Even the Chinese communists acknowledge Sun as a leader of the revolutionary movement that overthrew the imperial Manchu regime.[7] In response to the communists' political use of national reunification as a major theme of its psychological warfare against Taiwan after the withdrawal of U.S. diplomatic recognition of the ROC in 1979, the Nationalists have stated that only prior acceptance by the communists of Sun's three principles might constitute a framework of any future attempt at unification. Thus, a major political consideration has also been imparted to the ideological content of Sun's three principles, including the economic "principle of livelihood."

In order to improve the economic well-being of the people, Sun's doctrine calls for the "equalization of land ownership" and the exercise of a measure of government control over the unbridled rights of capital. Sun's economic ideas, therefore, contain a large element of egalitarianism with respect to the distribution of both wealth and income.

The need to create a national political consensus and to minimize divisiveness born of income disparity is an additional reason for the

ROC government's continuing concern about economic equality. A successful land reform in the early 1950s and an anti-poverty program among the urban and rural poor in the late 1960s and early 1970s constituted some of the major landmarks. The same interest in equity has drawn attention in economic discussions in Taiwan to measurements of inequality.[8] Equity figures prominently in policy discussions no less than in actual practice in many issues: for example, the consolidation of scattered parcels of farm land,[9] the mode of operation of large farms, the relative distribution of investment between the agricultural and nonagricultural sectors, measures to maintain farm prices and farm income, the incremental value tax on urban land, income tax reform, the preferential treatment of small business versus the encouragement of large-scale production, and the impact of new technology on rural income.[10] While these are economic issues by no means peculiar to Taiwan, weighing the equity aspects seriously while wrestling with problems of economic growth produces a qualitative difference between Taiwan and many other LDCs in economic policy making.

Economic and Price Stability

Another parameter of Taiwan's policy making is its sensitivity to price inflation and a paramount desire for stability. The heavy political cost the ROC government sustained in the years of hyperinflation in mainland China immediately before its withdrawal from the mainland and economic difficulties during the late 1940s and early 1950s in Taiwan gave the authorities an unusually strong desire for price stability and steady growth. While economists knowledgeable about conditions in Taiwan have differed on the extent fiscal and monetary conservatism has actually prevailed in practice, that unrestrained economic growth has never been pursued single-mindedly, at all cost, as it was for a time in the 1970s under the late President Park in South Korea and in some Latin American countries, seems quite indisputable.

The long-term objective of stable prices pursued at the cost of somewhat lower growth has come under re-examination from time to time for a number of reasons. First, the worldwide recession and decline of export growth and domestic investment have raised anew in Taiwan the age-old issues of monetary and interest rate policy. A major debate on the level of the interest rate and the degree to which the Central Bank should actively intervene in keeping it at certain prescribed levels was widely watched and reported in the daily press in Taiwan in the summer of 1982. Second, the desire for a more rapid growth of real GNP, which had fallen to 3.9 percent in 1982, a year of retrenchment, has been fostered partly by the underlying thought that a larger defense effort might be necessary to deter the PRC from military adventure against Taiwan. Finally, a nagging question is whether the secular growth rate of Taiwan has in fact peaked. If it has, then, as a developing economy, Taiwan must without further ado undergo certain major structural changes in order to move up from the plateau it had attained in the 1970s.

Over-anxiety about price stability may have had a particularly adverse effect in another way. When the price of crude oil rose sharply during the first oil crisis in the 1970s, in the interest of domestic price stability, Taiwan's utility rates were not raised to reflect fully the increase in fuel cost. The effects of this policy are somewhat debatable. On the one hand, one may well argue that the government budget received a jolt because of the subsidies the state-run oil refinery and power company received.[11] Besides, adjustments in energy use might have better reflected the real conditions of resource availability had the higher fuel and related cost increases been fully passed through. On the other hand, with the benefit of hindsight, one could also argue that this economically costly delay might nevertheless be politically justified, because too sharp price increases in early 1974, in response to the oil price increase, only two years after the Shanghai communiqué, might have been just too destabilizing politically. The issue is certainly debatable. The least one can say is that Taiwan's vulnerability as a resource-poor and import- as well as export-dependent economy faces a fundamental challenge: How quickly should it respond to large changes in external supply and/or demand in the future? Is structural distortion too high a price to pay for short-term stability? Is it always possible to recognize in good time permanent as against merely passing large external changes in demand and supply? How might a country like Taiwan increase its adaptability to unexpected external change?

Reaching a Plateau[12]

In 1982, according to CEPD estimates, the per capita GNP of Taiwan was NT $59,828 or US $1,529 at 1976 prices (NT $107,098 or U.S.

$2,673 at 1982 prices), which would put the ROC among the higher ranking middle income countries in the World Bank's tally. How the Taiwan economy has reached the present level of development has already been examined by a number of authors whose studies cover varying periods.[13] Since they wrote at different times, they differed somewhat in describing and explaining the paths of the economy's growth and its periodization. Nevertheless there is enough common ground on which most analysts would agree. In the following the reader's attention is drawn to a number of points which seem to be especially relevant to Taiwan's future economic growth.

First, the period between 1973 and 1975, when the impact of the first oil crisis of the 1970s was widely felt in many parts of the world, constituted a watershed in Taiwan's economic development. Until then the annual growth of GNP rose at a high and, on the average, steadily rising rate. Using as a unit of time the four-year period corresponding to Taiwan's indicative economic plan, real GNP, at constant 1976 prices, grew at the ascending rates in Table 1.2.

TABLE 1.2. Period Average of Annual Growth Rates of Real GNP (in percent)

Years	Percent	Increment in Percentage Points
1957-60	7.0	...
1961-64	9.1	+2.1
1965-68	9.9	+0.8
1969-72	11.6	+1.7

Source: Council for Economic Planning and Development, *Taiwan Statistical Data Book 1982*, (Taiwan: Executive Yuan, 1982).

The growth rate itself registered the largest acceleration in 1961-64, immediately preceding the termination of U.S. aid in 1965. A significant acceleration again occurred during 1969-72. As a matter of fact, the annual growth rate reached 13.3 percent in 1972 and was only slightly lower in 1973 (12.8 percent). However, the average real growth rate dropped to 5.9 percent in 1973-75; in 1974 it registered 1.1 percent only, the lowest annual growth on record since 1953. The shock of the oil price hike was so great that a new six-year prospective plan was drafted for 1976-81. Although the recovery rate was fairly rapid by world standards in the 1981-82 recession and Taiwan's real GNP never declined, the annual growth rates were only 5 percent in 1981 and 3.9 percent in 1982. The average of the growth rates fell to 9.5 percent in 1976-81. While the real growth rate rose further to 7.1 percent in 1983, the prospects of future growth and cyclical influence call for some serious soul-searching.

Second, the growth of output reflected a rapidly increasing productive capacity made possible by the continual expansion of the share of gross fixed capital formation in GNP. This ratio rose steadily during the successive four-year periods, from an average of 15.5 percent a year in 1957-60 and 15.4 percent in 1961-64 to 19.8 percent in 1965-68 and 22.9 percent in 1969-72. The share of gross fixed capital formation in GNP continued to rise even in 1973-75, thanks to a major push in government investment to modernize and expand the infrastructure of transportation, communications, and power supply.

Supporting the increase in capital formation has been that of gross savings. As may be seen in Table 1.3, while 1957-60 was the four-year period when the average ratio (average propensity to save) of gross savings in GNP went above 10 percent for the first time, it was in the following four-year period that the respective shares of gross savings and gross fixed capital formation became equal.

TABLE 1.3. Gross Savings and Gross Fixed Capital Formation (as percent of GNP)

	A Gross Savings	B Gross Fixed Capital Formation	A - B
1953-56	8.7	12.5	-3.8
1957-60	10.9	15.5	-4.6
1961-64	15.5	15.4	0.1
1965-68	21.4	19.8	1.6
1969-72	27.6	22.9	4.7
1973-75	31.1	28.5	2.6
1976-81	33.2	28.2	5.2

Source: Council for Economic Planning and Development, *Taiwan Statistical Data Book 1982*, (Taiwan: Executive Yuan, 1982).

The rise of savings in 1961–64 and the succeeding four-year periods made the financing of increasing investment far easier even though inventory building, which is normally between 2 and 4 percent of GNP, has not been included in the capital formation data in Table 1.3.

Third, the growth of Taiwan's economy was stimulated by rapidly rising export sales. During 1957–60, the average ratio of annual exports to GNP was 9.7 percent. It rose to 13.8 percent in 1961–64 and 29.3 percent in 1969–72. In 1972, when real GNP grew at the peak rate of 13.3 percent, exports were 38 percent of GNP. Even more notable is that in the post-oil crisis years of 1973–81, including 1973–75 when there was a sharp slow-down of growth, the share of exports in Taiwan's GNP continued to increase. In 1981, for every dollar of GNP, 48.7 cents were derived from exports.

That the home market is still too small to support Taiwan's rapidly expanding productive capacity is matched by the economy's dependence on imported raw materials and intermediate goods.[14] Hence growing exports have been accompanied by rapidly rising imports. The average of the annual import-to-GNP ratios in 1953–56 was 12.4 percent. It rose steadily to 20.9 percent in 1965–68. It was only in 1971 that the import-GNP ratio (at 28.2 percent) dipped below the year's export-GNP ratio (at 31.4 percent). In 1974, thanks to OPEC's price increases, imports again accounted for a larger proportion of GNP than exports (48.7 percent for imports and 39.2 percent for exports). This ratio was reversed once more in 1976; in 1981, the export-GNP and import-GNP ratios were 48.7 percent and 45.7 percent respectively.

Fourth, during the 17 years between 1965 and 1981, beginning from the time of U.S. aid termination, Taiwan had nine years of positive trade balances versus eight years of deficits. From 1971 onward, with the exception of 1974–75, the first two full years of the sharp oil price hikes of the 1970s, Taiwan has had a string of trade surpluses. The current account as a whole has been equally encouraging.

Fifth, the high levels of exports and domestic savings Taiwan has maintained have greatly reduced the problems of financing capital formation and balancing external payments many other developing countries have to face. As a result, external indebtedness[15] has been kept to a minimum and debt servicing does not present a major demand on foreign exchange earnings. With external credit in good standing, borrowing for major capital imports—for example, in building nuclear power plants and steel making—has not, therefore, presented any real problem. Otherwise, the replacement of the ROC by the PRC in the International Monetary Fund and the World Bank in 1980 might have had more far-reaching adverse effects than they actually did.

Nevertheless, foreign capital, especially in the form of direct private investment, has played an important role in Taiwan's economic development in several ways. Foreign investors who have set up plants in Taiwan to produce exportable goods, some in the country's several export-processing zones, have solved an export-marketing problem which might have been extremely hard to overcome initially by local exporters. Foreign investors have been instrumental in bringing with them new markets, as well as new technology and know-how. However limited may have been the further dissemination of this imported capability, its demonstration effect should not be underestimated. Finally, these investors and the pure traders have helped spread information about Taiwan all over the world, thus contributing to the island's rising international recognition.

Before 1973, the ratio of private foreign investment in gross domestic capital formation rose steadily, from only 1.6 percent in 1957-60 to 8.6 percent in 1969-72. The relative importance of private foreign capital rose fastest in the decade of the 1960s. After 1973, private foreign capital declined in importance, falling to an average ratio of only 2.9 percent of gross domestic capital formation in 1976-81. Nevertheless, the annual amount of private investment approvals in the last six-year period still averaged US $282.8 million as compared with $185.5 million in 1973-75.

Finally, for a resource-poor, external trade-oriented economy like Taiwan, the preceding record of sustained economic growth over about 30 years, including a period of rapid growth in 1961-73, could not have taken place without radical structural changes. These structural changes can be measured in many ways, such as the relative decline of the share of agricultural versus nonagricultural production; the continuous expansion of nonagricultural employment; within the nonagricultural sector, the increasing share of the manufacturing industry in capital formation; and, inevitably, the increasing share of manufactures in Taiwan's export list. Some of these data for 1964, 1973, and 1981 are presented in Table 1.4.

TABLE 1.4. Selected Indicators of Structural Change in the Taiwan Economy

	Ratio of Agricultural to Nonagricultural Net Domestic Products	Ratio of Agricultural to Nonagricultural Employment* (15 and over)	Manufacturing in Gross Domestic Capital Formation (percent)	Industrial Products in Total Exports (percent)
1964	1.0: 2.5	1.0:0.8	24.1	42.5
1973	1.0: 6.1	1.0:1.7	29.2	84.6
1981	1.0:10.5	1.0:2.5	28.7	92.2

*Including forestry and fisheries.

Source: Council for Economic Planning and Development, *Taiwan Statistical Data Book 1982* (Taiwan: Executive Yuan, 1982), pp. 9, 33, 41, and 189.

PROSPECTS FOR FURTHER GROWTH

The task confronting the Taiwan economy in 1983, when the economy in many debt-ridden developing countries was in dire straits but recovery in the country's main foreign market, the United States, had forged ahead, was to move up from the plateau to which it had clung during the recession abroad and to resume growth at a higher rate, hopefully even if expansion in the outside world should stall. This task involves both anticyclical policies in the short run and measures to boost the rate of secular growth in the long run. It is important that these short- and long-term policies be appropriately integrated. The question whether the expansion path traced by the Taiwan economy will succeed in moving from a "point of inflection" on to an exponential curve can be answered only after an examination from several different perspectives.

First, what objective conditions are necessary for the resumption of an increasing rate of growth? How are the problems posed by these conditions—and their realization—perceived by the decision makers in the government and the business community and among the working people at all levels, not to mention the academic analysts and social commentators whose views seem to be playing an increasing role in shaping policies in Taiwan? What practical measures have already been taken by the economic policy makers in advancing toward the perceived goals and in moving the economy and the private sector along the same path? Last but not least, how is the larger society in Taiwan adapting itself to the economic changes that have already occurred and will continue to take place, in terms of modifications of existing institutions and behavior so as to make the necessary change in the economy fast, successful, and smooth? Obviously, these questions cannot be answered all at once, yet it is to the extent that they can be answered satisfactorily that the Taiwan experience in continuing growth will be especially instructive to LDCs elsewhere and to students of economic development and social change.

In this connection we shall confine our discussion in the present chapter to two major points: namely, the external and internal conditions for the resumption of a higher growth rate.

Externally, we have already noted the increasing dependence of Taiwan on export as a source of demand for its growing output. During 1957-60, for every 1 percent increase in GNP, exports grew at an average rate of .6 percent. This ratio rose steadily to an average of 1.74 in 1969-72. In the years since 1973 it continued to rise, reaching an average of 2.42 during the six-year period of 1976-81. This means that under present conditions, for Taiwan's GNP to grow, it is necessary for exports to rise nearly two and one-half times faster. The problem is compounded by an equally increasing rate of growth of imports in raw materials and intermediate products. What are some of the possible underlying reasons for this phenomenon? Perhaps the prices of some of Taiwan's exports are too low. How can the dependence of GNP growth on trade be reduced? Given the dependence, how can the growth of foreign trade be accelerated? Perhaps the prices of some imports are too high—the cost of imported oil since 1973 is a case in point. The unfavorable terms of trade are tied to the nature of the commodities traded while the high import content in both exports and domestically traded goods reflects Taiwan's present state of technology and structure of production and the limited scope of import substitution. It would seem, therefore, that Taiwan must try to export more goods of a larger unit value and lower import content, which is to say a higher domestic value-added. For a country that is trade-dependent, reducing import content in its own production clearly should not be approached through protection against import but through increasing the efficiency and capacity of domestic production. The economy must undergo structural change and technological improvement.

Furthermore, even if Taiwan succeeds in reducing, relatively speaking, its dependence upon exports as a source of aggregate demand, it will still have to expand its overall exports. As an island economy, dependence upon external trade must be accepted as a fact of life. In this connection, therefore, it is necessary to make sure that the growth of export demand will not be frustrated by foreign protectionist policies or other forms of interruption from abroad. In order to reduce the effect of protectionist pressures in some importing countries, reduction of over-concentration in specific external markets and increasing diversification to other markets must accompany changes in the commodity composition of exports. Such an expansion in external trade relations needs to be accompanied by an increasing internationalization of Taiwan's developing multi-faceted relations with other countries, both regionally and in areas farther away. The multinational development of Taiwan's external economic and other relationships will also help in safeguarding the island's transportation and trade links with the rest of the world.

Commodity trade alone is not all that matters. Other items on the current account of the country's balance of payments should receive attention. By this we mean the growth of foreign exchange earnings from the export of "factor service." Currently Taiwan's already well-known construction engineering service constitutes one such export. Perhaps other comparable service exports will emerge. One would assume that eventually a net inflow of dividend and interest income can be developed once investments based on export surpluses can be built up. Available information suggests that a few Taiwan firms have already begun to establish subsidiaries in foreign countries, including Indonesia, Thailand, and other countries in the region, as well as in the United States.

Increasing the value-added of Taiwan's exports, lowering the import content of the country's products without protection and changing the structure of the economy—all this will be predicated upon new technologies, new resources, and changes in the methods and organization of production and foreign sales. These changes on the supply side require in turn an inward transfer of the fruits of foreign research and development (R&D) and the wide dissemination of new imported and indigenous technologies. Where transfers of foreign technology and research results cannot be separated from foreign capital, foreign investments and the licensing of foreign technology will have to be promoted.

Internally, one of the adverse developments in the 1970s has been the rise of the real wage rate at a faster pace than that of labor productivity in manufacturing. For instance, while the real wage in manufacturing rose during 1973 and 1975 at 17.3 percent and 13 percent respectively, direct labor productivity fell by 0.6 percent in 1973 and increased by only 5.7 percent in 1975. In 1974, the real wage fell by 9 percent while direct labor productivity in manufacturing dropped by 9.5 percent. Again, in two of the four years between 1976 and 1979 inclusive, direct labor productivity either fell or grew at a lower rate than real wage. This declining rate of increase in labor productivity will have to be corrected if Taiwan is to maintain its competitiveness and the correction must come from increasing investment and/or the application of new or improved technology. Accordingly it is necessary to keep the rate of savings high, to mobilize available savings for the financing of productive investment and to develop means of effective dissemination of new technology. All this implies that the necessary incentives and institutions must be in place and that both public and private economic and related behavior must undergo the necessary adjustments to change.

The prospects of growth in the long run will ultimately depend upon a high degree of adaptability on the part of the people in Taiwan. The latter boils down ultimately to a matter of individual and collective behavior, a question of values and how determined Taiwan, as a nation, will be to uphold them.

It follows from the above that the principal issues and tasks facing the ROC authorities on Taiwan can be summed up under several headings:

Greater Internationalization of the Economy

1. Further expansion of exports through quality upgrading and diversification by commodity and by country;
2. Progressive liberalization of imports so that the country can enjoy the economic benefits of cheap imports as well as the political advantage of bargaining against foreign protectionist measures aimed at Taiwan's products;

3. Greater integration of the Taiwan economy in the world economy as a regional center of transshipment, warehousing, and intra-regional commerce and finance;
4. Encouragement of greater capital interflows between Taiwan and the rest of the world for the purpose of increasing the inflow of embodied foreign technology and the long-run accumulation of ROC investments abroad in order to assure future supply and to build up future external income.

Coordination of Development, R&D, Education, and Manpower Policies

1. Further development of domestic legislation and of an environment conducive to the inflow of embodied foreign technology;
2. Adjustment of the domestic R&D, higher education, and vocational training systems so that the dissemination, adaptation, and commercialization of imported technology and of indigenously developed technology can be expedited;
3. Development of a manpower policy that will assure supply of the requisite R&D, managerial, and technical personnel for the country's development while providing an outlet for the external investment of Taiwan's surplus skilled manpower in foreign countries in the long run.
4. The uninterrupted acquisition and development of knowledge about foreign countries and of linguistic, legal, marketing, and other relevant skills to deal with the rest of the world.

Mobilization of Resources for Growth and Structural Change

1. Further development of the existing structure of financial institutions, including especially banks and the capital market (a) to mobilize savings from all sectors of the economy and (b) to provide access by all the savers to investments in all sectors, including, in the long run, investment in foreign assets;
2. With growth, the development of an economic structure that will be readily responsive to changes in world demand so that the size of the domestic market, which tends to lag behind the growth of

APPENDIX TABLE 1.1. Economic Growth Rates and Indicators of Structural Change, 1953–1981 (in percent per year unless otherwise noted)

	1953	1954	1955	1956	1957	1958	1959	1960	1961	1962	1963	1964	1965	1966	1967	1968	1969	1970	1971	1972	1973	1974	1975	1976	1977	1978	1979	1980	1981
Growth (annual rate)																													
GNP (1976 prices)	9.3	9.6	8.1	5.5	7.3	6.6	7.7	6.5	6.8	7.8	9.4	12.3	11.0	9.0	10.6	9.1	9.0	11.3	12.9	13.3	12.8	1.1	4.2	13.5	9.9	13.9	8.1	6.6	5.0
Agricultural production	9.4	2.1	0.5	7.6	7.1	6.6	1.6	1.4	8.8	2.8	0.2	12.0	6.4	3.3	6.4	6.8	-2.0	5.5	0.5	2.2	2.6	2.0	-1.2	10.0	4.0	-1.8	5.3	-11.0	-0.6
Industrial production	25.0	6.0	13.2	3.3	12.9	8.6	11.8	14.1	15.5	8.0	9.1	21.2	16.3	15.6	16.7	22.3	19.9	20.1	24.7	21.2	16.2	-4.5	8.5	24.4	13.6	22.8	8.0	7.3	4.0
Manufacturing production	33.3	6.8	10.6	5.8	14.5	7.9	13.2	14.3	12.5	8.1	9.3	23.1	16.7	16.1	17.4	24.9	22.7	22.2	26.6	22.7	17.7	-6.0	8.0	25.6	13.4	26.1	6.9	8.7	4.0
Exports	35.1	-26.9	32.1	52.9	25.4	5.1	47.8	4.5	30.9	11.8	52.1	30.7	3.6	19.3	19.5	23.2	33.0	41.2	39.1	45.0	42.8	25.2	-5.7	53.8	14.6	31.9	23.6	22.9	16.5
Imports	8.7	20.0	-4.8	52.6	9.6	6.6	50.2	28.2	19.4	-5.6	19.0	18.5	29.9	11.9	29.5	12.1	34.3	25.7	21.0	36.3	43.9	82.9	-14.7	27.7	12.0	26.1	30.5	33.5	9.4
Population	3.8	3.7	3.8	3.4	3.2	3.6	3.9	3.5	3.3	3.3	3.2	3.1	3.0	2.9	2.3	2.7	5.0	2.4	2.2	2.0	1.8	1.8	1.9	2.2	1.8	1.9	2.0	1.9	1.6
Direct labor productivity in manufacturing	—	—	—	—	—	—	—	—	—	—	—	—	—	—	—	26.0	10.2	9.2	15.2	5.3	-0.6	-9.5	5.7	17.2	4.7	15.3	-2.1	3.3	3.3
Structural Change																													
Nonagricultural employment (annual rate of growth)	0.2	4.1	2.1	0.4	7.5	5.0	4.0	3.4	3.4	3.4	4.9	3.3	2.2	4.7	14.7	5.1	23.8	3.5	11.7	11.2	9.6	3.1	3.9	9.1	4.2	7.9	7.8	3.2	4.7
Gross savings as percent of GNP	8.9	7.7	9.0	9.2	10.6	9.9	10.3	12.7	12.8	12.4	17.1	19.6	19.6	21.5	22.5	22.1	23.8	25.5	28.8	32.1	34.6	31.7	26.9	32.5	33.0	35.2	34.6	33.3	31.4
Gross fixed capital formation as percent of GNP	11.7	13.3	11.4	13.4	13.2	15.2	16.7	16.7	16.3	15.2	15.4	14.7	17.1	19.2	20.7	22.1	22.3	21.8	23.4	23.9	25.1	28.8	31.5	28.1	26.1	26.3	28.6	31.3	28.5
Private foreign investment as percent of gross domestic capital formation	1.6	0.9	1.8	1.6	0.6	0.8	0.4	4.5	4.1	1.5	4.5	4.2	6.5	4.4	6.4	8.5	9.1	9.6	9.4	6.3	8.0	3.4	2.5	2.5	2.7	2.8	3.0	3.4	3.0
Investment in manufacturing as percent of gross fixed capital formation	22.9	23.9	20.5	24.2	26.6	24.1	20.6	23.5	22.5	21.6	22.7	31.0	29.8	29.8	33.7	33.4	32.4	36.1	31.1	32.8	34.0	38.1	39.0	37.0	29.5	24.5	27.5	30.1	30.3
Exports as percent of GNP	8.7	5.8	6.4	8.6	9.2	8.7	11.1	9.6	11.2	11.4	15.3	17.1	16.1	17.1	17.7	18.7	21.4	26.3	31.4	38.0	41.9	39.2	34.7	44.5	43.8	48.4	49.7	49.4	48.7
Imports as percent of GNP	12.0	13.2	10.5	14.0	13.2	12.6	16.4	17.4	18.5	15.9	16.7	16.9	19.9	19.9	22.3	21.5	24.8	27.1	28.2	32.1	35.6	48.7	39.0	41.5	39.9	42.2	45.8	49.4	45.7
Trade balance as percent of GNP	-3.4	-7.4	-4.1	-5.5	-4.0	-3.9	-5.3	-7.8	-7.3	-4.5	-1.4	0.2	-3.9	-2.8	-4.6	-2.8	-3.4	-0.8	3.2	6.0	6.3	-9.5	-4.3	3.0	3.9	6.2	4.0	0.1	3.0

Source: Council for Economic Planning and Development, *Taiwan Statistical Data Book 1982*, (Taiwan: Executive Yuan, 1982).

aggregate demand, will not become a source of vested interest militating against innovation and adaptation;
3. In conjunction with the preceding point, the institution of lifetime continuing education and technical training programs so as to enhance the adaptability and occupational mobility of the work force.

Enhancement of the Quality of Life and the Continued Improvement of Distributive Equity

1. Minimization of the external social costs and diseconomies of growth due to conglomeration, over-urbanization, industrial pollution, and other adverse effects of economic growth;
2. A sustained watch over any adverse impact of growth on inequality of opportunity and of income that might undermine the national consensus and the cohesiveness of the population;
3. Consolidation of the country's traditional values (including its work ethic) and the enhancement of new values conducive to steady economic growth in a socially stable environment. This is perhaps the most fundamental task of all.

NOTES

1. The World Bank, *World Development Report, 1979* (New York: Oxford University Press, 1979), pp. 87 and 88. Interestingly, the World Bank, like the International Monetary Fund, has deferred to the PRC, a member of both institutions since 1980 in place of the ROC, by not mentioning Taiwan in any published material since 1980!

2. For an account of U.S. policy during the years leading to U.S. withdrawal from Southeast Asia, see Wu, Yuan-li, *U.S. Policy and Strategic Interests in the Western Pacific* (New York: Crane, Russak, 1975).

3. Under the Carter administration (1977–80), the term "parallel strategic interest" became a popular argument used by U.S. advocates of closer cooperation with the PRC, that is, against a common Soviet adversary, short of an open alliance. The concept was carried over into the Reagan administration by the foreign policy establishment until 1982 when George Schultz became secretary of state.

4. The United States announced in December 1978 the switch of diplomatic recognition from the ROC to the PRC as of the beginning of 1979.

5. Countries like the Phillippines and Malaysia have the additional problems facing primary commodity exporters but they also have greater leeway in import

substitution. Taiwan, on the other hand, has neither the problem nor the opportunity. Sugar export is probably an exception.

6. According to Article One of the Chinese Constitution, "The Republic of China, founded on the Three Principles of the People, [that is, Sun Yat-sen's political philosophy] should be a democratic republic of the people to be governed by the people and for the people." See *China Yearbook 1978* (Taipei: China Publishing, 1978), p. 647. For an interesting recent discussion on the principle of livelihood, see C. L. Sheng, "New Interpretation of Dr. Sun Yat-sen's Philosophy of the People's Livelihood," *Renaissance Monthly* (Taipei), No. 152, May 1984, pp. 5-18.

7. See, for instance, Mao, Tse-tung (Mao Zedong), "In Commemoration of Dr. Sun Yat-sen," in *Selected Works* (Peking: Foreign Language Press, 1977), Vol. V, p. 330.

8. See, for instance, Kuo, Shirley, W. Y., *The Taiwan Economy in Transition* (Boulder, CO: Westview Press, 1983). For a discussion on the anti-poverty program, see Wu, Yuan-li and Yeh, Kung-chia, eds., *Growth, Distribution, and Social Change; Essays on the Economy of the Republic of China* (University of Maryland: School of Law, 1978), Occasional Papers/Reprints Series in Contemporary Asian Studies No. 3 (15), 1978, pp. 67-111. The same consideration underlies the ROC's consistent policy to maintain a viable agricultural sector and a high level of domestic food production in spite of the apparently greater comparative advantage of manufacturing.

9. This is sometimes described as a second land reform in contrast to the first land reform which created owner-farmers and reduced tenant farming.

10. Yung-peng Chu and Tien-wang Tsaur, "Growth, Stability and Income Distribution in Taiwan." Paper presented at Western Social Science Association meeting, San Diego, CA, April 1984.

11. In 1974, the "surplus of public enterprises and public utilities" constituted 8.6 percent of total consolidated government revenue, declining from 14.1 percent a year earlier. During the same year electricity rates were raised by 78.7 percent, fuel oil by 88.4 percent, while crude oil prices rose by an average of 185.5 percent. *Industry of Free China* 55, 5 (May 1981): 13 (Chinese section).

12. See Appendix Table 1.1.

13. Wu and Yeh, *Growth, Distribution and Social Change*; Lin, Ching-yuan, *Industrialization in Taiwan, 1946-72: Trade and Import-Substitution Policies for Developing Countries* (New York: Praeger, 1973) (Praeger Special Studies in International Economics and Development); Yü, Chung-hsien, ed., *Taiwan Chingchi Fachan Tsunglun* [An Introduction to Taiwan's Economic Development] (Taipei: Lienching, 1975); Kuo, Shriley, W. Y., Gustav Ranls, and John C. H. Fei, *The Taiwan Success Story: Rapid Growth with Improved Distribution in the Republic of China, 1952-1979* (Boulder, CO: Westview Press, 1981); Ho, Samuel, P. S., *Economic Development of Taiwan 1980-1970* (New Haven: Yale University Press, 1978).

14. This is an important aspect in which the more developed Japanese economy differs from that of Taiwan. Japan, like Taiwan, is dependent upon imported raw materials and fuel but, unlike Taiwan, is much less dependent upon imported intermediate goods and capital equipment.

15. According to the Asian Development Bank, Taiwan's debt service ratio (that is, service payments on external public debt as percentage of exports of goods and all services including workers' remittances) was 4.0 percent in 1979. For 1977, the World Bank gave 4.3 percent for Taiwan as compared with 9.2 percent for all "middle income countries." See The World Bank, *World Development Report, 1979* (Washington, D.C.: Oxford University Press, 1979), p. 151; Asian Development Bank, *Key Indicators of Developing Member Countries of ADB* 13, No. 1 (April 1982), p. 32.

2

AN EVOLVING ECONOMIC STRATEGY AND CONSENSUS

So far, the issues facing the Taiwan economy as an NIC eager to accelerate its advance on a path of continuing growth have been enumerated from the standpoint of an observer looking at Taiwan primarily as a small open economy that has more or less fully utilized its initially abundant supply of semi-skilled labor and its inherently limited natural resource endowment. Hence, in the long run, the issues that must be resolved inevitably revolve around the creation of new comparative advantages that could give the economy a growing but changing role in the world economy so that its population can aspire to a rising income and production not quickly susceptible to diminishing returns.

The deductive reasoning of an outsider does not necessarily correspond to the perception of policy makers. Furthermore, an economist examining a small number of macroeconomic problems, looking for trends and solutions, tends to overlook the many real, practical obstacles on the way. He is prone, therefore, to underestimate the length of time needed in the evolution of a comprehensive policy of economic development. Even the most far-ranging and carefully thought-out policy on paper would be of no use if it could not be implemented. Successful implementation is more likely if the policy can win general acceptance, which entails understanding and approval on the part of the public. Accordingly, we shall devote this chapter, first, to an account of the manner in which a national economic policy for continued growth has evolved at the turn of the decade,[1] followed by an examination of the views of some academicians and businessmen. The discussion will deal with the thrust of both general economic policy and, as one of its principal components, R&D policy and the promotion of technology- or knowledge-intensive industries in particular.

ECONOMIC GOALS AND POLICY EMPHASIS BEFORE 1979

The severance of formal diplomatic relations by the United States with the Republic of China on Taiwan dealt a severe blow to the latter and thus became a watershed in Taiwan's economic policy. What is surprising, however, is the degree of continuity ROC economic policy has maintained since 1979 in spite of the new challenge occasioned by the change in external environment. In order to understand the initially rather subtle but subsequently much more far-reaching responses to the new situation on the part of Taiwan's leaders in their economic program, the stated policy goals of the ROC government some time before December 1978 should be compared with announced policies in 1979 and thereafter.

On February 25, 1977, about a month after President Carter's inauguration, Chiang Ching-kuo, then head of the Executive Yuan[2] (that is, Premier), told the ROC legislature that the economic goals of his administration continued to be the growth of the national economic potential so that the population would enjoy a higher standard of living and a better quality of life. Greater investment in the infrastructure[3] through the initiation of ten major construction projects and promotion of investment in general would therefore continue as before. Furthermore, development would be pursued in an open economy and under the condition of price stability. The government was, however, ready to intervene both in pump-priming in order to encourage private investment and in price stabilization in the face of any development that it might regard as monopolistic or manipulative by distributors. Shortly afterwards, in a budget message to the Legislature on April 8, 1977,[4] Premier Chiang stressed the importance of balancing government expenditure and revenue as a means of assuring stability. Thus both the long-term goals and the principal policy options were unchanged; they were the same time-honored policies that stood the test in the preceding decade of rapid development and of adjustment in 1974–75 in the aftermath of the first oil shock.

On a sectoral basis, Chiang Ching-kuo's February 1977 policy statement envisaged (1) the vigorous promotion of capital- and technology-intensive industries, together with, however, (2) maximum assistance to the existing labor-intensive enterprises in terms of management, equipment renewal, and efforts to increase labor productivity. The government further announced (3) its intention to increase rural investment and to promote agricultural mechanization, improvements in food production, marketing of agricultural products, and agricultural R&D. Finally, (4) Chiang's policy message spoke of the objective to develop a more rounded industrial structure that would enable Taiwan to create a greater "layer" of intermediate industries between imported resources and the production of final products for either domestic consumption or foreign trade.

In promoting external trade, the government focused its attention in the February 1977 statement on marketing and trade information. It called for the establishment of large trading companies modelled after those of the Japanese. It announced its plan to establish a world trade center as a permanent institution to bring together foreign buyers and sellers with those of Taiwan. It called for greater attention on the part of private business to quality control, business standards and business reputation, all of which had become matters of increasing concern.

The government, which obviously realized the need for change in the country's industrial structure, nevertheless at this time envisaged the change required as a gradual process during which the labor-intensive industries could stay competitive in world trade through improvements in labor productivity and marketing. Moreover, the structural change was to lead to the establishment of both capital and technology-intensive industries. Included in the backward linkage were chemical and heavy industries.

The development of certain industries to meet national defense needs was mentioned in the September 1977 message of the prime minister to the Legislature.[5] Both the September 1977 and the February 1978[6] policy statements described plans to revise the statute on investments in order to offer more inducements to investors through tax relief, cheaper and easier credit, and encouragement of business mergers. These somewhat recurrent emphases aside, the ROC government's policy was to stay on course. The overall slogan remained "growth with stability" or "stability in growth." If there was a change at all, it was perhaps a slightly greater emphasis on growth than before, a subtle movement at the most.

INCREASING EMPHASIS ON SCIENCE AND TECHNOLOGY (S&T)

The main goals of Taiwan's economic policy remained unchanged when Y. S. Sun became Premier in 1978 after the election of Chiang Ching-kuo to the presidency.[7] In his September 1978 message to the Sixty-second session of the Legislature, Sun, who had been Chiang Ching-kuo's Minister of Economic Affairs, reaffirmed the nation's dual economic goals as growth and equity. By equity he meant the further narrowing of the income gap between the rich and the poor.[8] Among the priorities listed were strengthening of defense, development of technology-intensive industries, and agricultural modernization. New emphasis was given to two areas. First, Sun wanted more efficient management in monetary and fiscal affairs, including the simplification and more effective collection of taxes, stricter control of investment trusts and insurance companies and improved banking operations. Second, he was explicit in stating manpower planning goals, shifting the government's primary emphasis from employment to the upgrading of technical skills and the more efficient use of available manpower. The demand for skills was to be matched by supply. At the lower level this meant more vocational training and employment guidance, beginning already at the level of the junior high school. At the higher end of the manpower spectrum, Sun asked for a rapid increase in S&T manpower. Among the specific measures proposed in this regard were cooperation between business and educational institutions, better division of labor and sharing in information collection among the R&D institutions, encouragement of R&D activities by private firms, greater emphasis on R&D in state enterprises, a planned approach to the importation of R&D results from abroad and their permanent absorption in Taiwan, the promotion of international cooperation in research, and, finally, the establishment of a Science-based Industry Park (S.I.P.) at Hsinchu where several graduate research institutes in science and technology were already located.

A POLICY OF REINVIGORATED GROWTH AND INTERNATIONALIZATION

We have dwelled at some length on the ROC's economic policy on the eve of the rupture of formal U.S.-ROC diplomatic ties in order to place in clear relief the nature of Taiwan's economic policy since 1979. The policy expounded by Premier Sun in September 1978 may well be regarded as a transitional step between the normal developmental policy which the open economy of Taiwan, as one of the successful Asian NICs, can be expected to pursue and a more vigorous and concerted effort to reinforce and accelerate structural change in the Taiwan economy in order to face the far greater external challenge that was now expected. In the end, a policy aimed at development cum security came to be developed over a period of several years. The priority items were announced first, as one might well expect. These were followed by the identification of longer term developmental requirements. The latter happen to coincide with those conditions under which the Taiwan economy could begin to gain new comparative advantages.

The first set of policy measures announced by Premier Sun immediately after the diplomatic rupture aimed at assuring Taiwan of critical supplies.[9] Among these measures were (1) building of emergency stocks based on estimates of domestic production, import, consumption and export; (2) as a new long-run measure, encouragement of selected investments abroad to assure future supply; (3) as an integral part of the preceding general policy, the formulation of an energy supply, consumption, and conservation policy that includes making investments abroad to develop future sources of energy import.

In the same February 1979 message, the machinery (including specifically the automotive), electronics, and selected chemical industries were singled out as priority or "strategic industries" to be given special preference. The list was subsequently modified to include industries producing certain special materials used in manufacturing while the microelectronic and computer industries were grouped under the broad term "information industry" to cover various forms of computer use, including computer-aided design and manufacturing. By 1983 the information industry, centered on computer hardware as well as software, together with automation, had become the focal point of the government's drive toward the restructuring of Taiwan's industrial sector. As a matter of fact, it has become a household phrase, the "buzz-word" in public statements. Plans for the information industry as an avantgarde of the entire high-technology sector are intimately tied to a program of education, training, and recruitment of scientists, engineers, technicians, and management personnel. Development of the underlying principles has, however, taken time and deserves more attention later.

Externally, aside from the security of critical supplies from abroad, Y. S. Sun made the development of multiple economic ties between Taiwan and the rest of the world the central theme of his administration's foreign economic policy. The individual policy components were summed up in an oral presentation by Sun in February, 1983 before the Seventy-first session of the Legislative Yuan.[10] The principal items consisted of

1. Development of Taiwan's harbors, including port facilities at Kaohsiung and Taichung, for purposes of intraregional transshipment by containers and of bulk cargo;
2. Expansion of passenger and cargo traffic and of new routes by the national China Air Lines linking Taiwan to European and additional U.S. and other cities;
3. The opening up of Taiwan's security market to foreign investors in the form of depository receipts;
4. Development of offshore banking and of a free trade area in addition to the export processing zones which had been a leading contribution of Taiwan emulated by other LDCs desiring trade expansion, including the PRC.

The formal opening of the Hsinchu Science-based Industry Park in December 1980 and the construction of a World Trade Center can be regarded as the two most visible physical symbols of Taiwan's economic policy at this stage of its development. The two projects are also representative of the ROC's response to the U.S. abrogation of the 1954 Mutual Defense Treaty with Taiwan in 1979 and the PRC's deliberate and continuing efforts to isolate Taiwan politically and economically. However, while the emphasis given to the development of high technology industries and intensified internationalization of the economy have been unprecedented, they really constitute the further strengthening of existing trends. Many novel approaches appear to have been devised to add substance to policies which, if our analysis in the introductory chapter is not mistaken, are what a small open economy short of natural resources like Taiwan should in fact try to do at this stage of its development. These specific measures have lent practicality and meaning to principles of economic development that might otherwise prove rather arid and vacuous except to theorists in economics.

One sectoral emphasis in Premier Sun's successive policy statements, however, stands out as a long-standing, almost traditional, feature that should be pointed out. This is the unwavering objective of increasing rural real income and of keeping the gap between urban and rural incomes within a hopefully narrowing range. Government funds totalling hundreds of millions of NT dollars have been appropriated for rural public investment. This has been accompanied by a farm policy which deliberately keeps agriculture from declining relatively as much as it might otherwise do.

ISSUES IN IMPLEMENTATION

The series of economic policy reports emmanating from the Prime Minister's office at six-month intervals deal with the nation's long- and short-term objectives and principal policies in broad strokes. They reflect the perceptions of ROC leaders. Most of the policies—with the exception of some aspects of the agricultural program—are probably above controversy. However, this is not to say that unforeseen issues have not arisen or that some of the anticipated problems have not turned out to be more stubborn than expected. In particular, where an optional balance has to be scored between alternatives, a consensus must be reached before a policy that enjoys general approval in its broad outline can be fully implemented in detail.

As of 1983, a major portion of the industrial program was administered by the Ministry of Economic Affairs. The same ministry is also a principal actor in creating a hospitable investment climate. In order to secure maximum cooperation from the private sector, consensus was needed on the following issues:[11]

1. Balancing industry and agriculture. The ROC government, according to then Economic Affairs Minister Y. T. Chao, appreciated the importance of agriculture as a source of food and industrial raw materials, as well as of employment; but agriculture was de-

clining relatively and some representatives of the public thought that more weight should be given to the agricultural sector.
2. Comparative advantage versus protection. Chao pointed to the demand for protection by vested interests in industries that had lost their international competitiveness. Giving in to such demands would condemn users of the protected higher-priced domestic products to an inferior competitive position in the world and be detrimental to domestic consumer interests as well.
3. Government-run enterprises and the private sector. In Chao's opinion, the government should encourage private investment and offer guidance, information, and other assistance to investors in new fields of high risk. Beyond that, the government should limit its own enterprises to petroleum, electric power, steel, and sugar, all of which were already, and still are, run by state enterprises.
4. Domestic versus foreign capital. Taiwan's modernization would require the full participation of foreign capital, technology, and management. This could not be accomplished if the Taiwan economy remained narrowly "nationalistic."
5. Large versus small scale enterprises. There was, according to Chao, an erroneous interpretation of the "principle of people's livelihood"; to wit, that it distrusted large-scale private business and identified the latter with monopoly. Chao would prefer to keep under control any tendency toward monopoly through the competition imports would offer.
6. Short-term versus long-term economic interests. Short-term interests, according to Chao, emphasize the need for government to help maintain the status quo, including the preservation of enterprises that should be eliminated by competition. Long-term interest demands that the necessary structural change be facilitated rather than held up.
7. Deliberate planning of large-scale investment versus trendy small-scale investments. As large-scale investments become necessary for optimal operation, potential entrepreneurs should avoid the thoughtless pursuit of trendy investments which are common in the Taiwan business community and have often resulted in cut-throat competition.

Expanding on the same points in an address in March 1983,[12] the Economics Minister again stressed the urgency of (1) relying on the price mechanism to reflect relative scarcity; (2) bringing outdated legal statutes and regulatory measures affecting the economy up to date; (3) strengthening S&T by developing the information industry, automation, and international industrial cooperation; (4) modernizing management to match the advance of S&T; (5) establishing an orderly system of large and small enterprises; and (6) increasing the training of sophisticated manpower. In particular, Chao urged more long-term risk taking by private entrepreneurs, and a more accelerated pace in adjusting the industrial structure so as not to miss the anticipated worldwide recovery of demand.

The above observations by a key official responsible for the implementation of most economic policy suggest that while Taiwan needs large-scale private investment in new knowledge-intensive industries, which on occasion—but not necessarily always—are capital-intensive, the private sector has been less than eager to invest in new and untried fields. The government, on the other hand, which was in 1983 weighed down by some loss-ridden state enterprises (for example, the government owned Taiwan Metal and Taiwan Aluminum companies) should discard them and concentrate its effort on operating just four such enterprises and giving help to the private sector by guiding it toward more promising fields, thereby promoting the much desired structural change.

STREAMLINING THE FISCAL ADMINISTRATION AND FINANCIAL INSTITUTIONS

Equally interesting and enlightening were the thoughts of the then Finance Minister Hsü Li-teh when he spoke to the press at the beginning of 1983.[13] Minister Hsü's immediate concerns were as follows:

1. More efficient use of funds under the control of the Ministry in order to promote investment;
2. More efficient use of all government-owned assets;
3. More effective income tax collection, including broadening of the tax base and plugging loopholes;
4. Introduction of a value-added tax, together with the necessary adjustments of the existing sales, stamp, and excise taxes;
5. Better collection of customs duties, together with a broad reduction of tariff rates and the progressive abolition of import tariff rebates enjoyed by exporters on their imported inputs;

6. Devising appropriate controls for trust companies and government-owned banks in a general policy of liberalization of the banking system and the capital market.

Under item (1), monies have already been appropriated for use in extending special development loans through the Bank of Communications' Development Loan Fund. As of the beginning of 1983, the establishment of another special loan fund for smaller business firms ("medium-sized and small businesses" in Taiwan's usage) was planned; other such funds may be forthcoming. Minister Hsü was obviously thinking in terms of the optimal use of government funds for medium- and long-term capital investment that were designed for special purposes and to reach segments of the economy not having adequate access to the supply of capital. In mid-1983 Minister Hsü visited the United States to explore potential external sources of venture capital for investment in Taiwan. These steps were complemented by efforts to tighten public control over the securities exchange and to admit trading in depository certificates of selected stocks by foreign buyers.

It is of more than passing interest that two of Taiwan's principal cabinet members responsible for the health of the economy were preoccupied simultaneously with (1) the philosophical problem of finding the optimal combinations of public and private enterprise, large and small business, free trade and protection of selected industries and domestic and foreign capital, and the proper integration of short-term interest in the level of economic activity with long-term concerns about reinvigorated and accelerated growth; and (2) the practical problems of collecting more taxes and using government-controlled monies more effectively and purposefully. It is not accidental that the Minister of Economic Affairs was primarily concerned with the first set of issues while the person holding the portfolio of the Treasury would fret about the best way to raise and disburse funds for the government. Some overlapping aside, the issues discussed so far are unquestionably among the core problems that must be resolved. How the first set of questions will be resolved will affect the answers to the second set.[14]

THE PUBLIC-PRIVATE SECTOR DIALOGUE

Lagging private investment in the first years of the 1980s[15] were deplored by many. Yu Kuo-hwa, who became Prime Minister in 1984—

Y. S. Sun had been felled by sudden illness—spoke out in January 1983 as Chairman of the ROC's Council for Economic Planning and Development and concurrently Governor of the Central Bank on what he hoped the private sector would do.[16] Yu appealed to Taiwan's entrepreneurs to recognize that adjustment would be painful. The far-sighted entrepreneur, said Yu, should go all out to gather commercial intelligence, improve management, and make timely investments in new equipment, R&D, and novel ventures. Coupled with this appeal, Yu pledged the government's continued effort to create a hospitable investment climate, to improve the efficiency of economic administration, to liberalize the financial institutions and to rationalize the tax system. These were the same measures the Economics and Finance Ministries emphasized.

On their side, some of Taiwan's most successful entrepreneurs have made clear the kind of institutional adjustments they would most like to see. Ku Cheng-fu, for instance, speaks of the need for consensus among private businessmen over investment in large-scale entreprises for the long pull and the social responsibility of private business.[17] To him structural change implies not only the introduction of new capital equipment and technology, but also the transformation of family-owned into public-owned business, the capacity for self-generation of new products and new technologies, the continuous improvement of the productivity and skill of technical labor, and better international marketing. While the business community appreciates the government's efforts in devising new measures designed to encourage investment, especially through favorable tax and credit adjustments, it is even more interested, according to Ku, in the presence of some other effective factors that make for a favorable investment climate. Among these, Ku lists: a healthy capital and money market, an effective monetary policy, high efficiency in administration, and an educational and training system commensurate with the rapid development of science and technology. Because of the large investments and/or high risks of new high-technology capital-intensive ventures, Ku asks especially for the kind of unambiguous legal standards and public discipline of an open society that would minimize the arbitrary element in evaluating such investment. It appears that thoughtful and respectable representatives of Taiwan's business community are looking beyond the more obvious incentives to investment like favorable taxes and credits.[18] They ask for less ambiguity and more openness in the government's industrial policy and priorities.

Some of the hesitance and seeming lack of sure-footedness in economic policy actually reflects the lack of consensus on some of the points raised by the Economics Minister. Consensus-building is necessary when radical changes are demanded by the political and economic challenges Taiwan faces. Yet consensus building is a function of time and persuasion through open discussion. One good example of such open discussion was a public forum in mid-1982.

THE INTEREST RATE, MONEY SUPPLY, AND EQUITY-DEBT RATIO—A TRIPARTITE DEBATE

Although the exact nature of the institutional framework is a central problem in consensus building, the unsettled state of changing institutions should not be held alone responsible for Taiwan's lagging investments during 1981-82 when falling world demand and high energy prices were depressing the country's external market. Hence a separate debate raged during this period around several continuing monetary issues. One side advocates some relaxation of credit while professing concern for price stability and the undesirability of unbridled monetary expansion, arguing that the real rate of interest in Taiwan had been too high. The other side stresses (1) that the nominal rate of interest was high (in the summer of 1981) only because of continuing inflation, (2) that inflation could not be controlled unless the growth of money supply were kept under control, (3) that determination of the interest rate should be left to the market, and that once inflation has been arrested, the real rate of interest would fall of its own accord, thus resuscitating private investment. The latter group makes two additional points. First, inflation is taxation without representation and has an uneven impact on persons at different levels of income, generally speaking, favoring the rich. Second, credit expansion—presumably long-term loans in particular—would further augment the debt-equity ratio of Taiwan firms, freeing the owners' funds for use elsewhere and exposing borrowed funds, largely from government banks, to risks the owners did not wish to bear themselves. As one can readily imagine, advocates of the first group consisted of some academicians and most businessmen while the second group was made up of the ROC's monetarists and other academicians.

As usual, such debates tend to be muddled by uncertain facts—whether the nominal rate of interest was x percent and whether the inflation rate was y percent, and so on.[19] They tend to become confused by frequent shifts of the question from what the Central Bank should do to what it did on past occasions. Understandably, the last point contributed to a great deal of heated discussion between the contestants.

From the perspective of an outside neutral observer, the important point is that such a public debate not only took place in Taiwan, but did so in an open forum with a great deal of public fanfare and participation. The *Commercial Times,* sponsor of the forum on August 18, 1982, prefaced the day's meeting in which six outstanding business leaders and eight noted academic economists participated, by stressing the importance of consensus building in support of the resurgence of Taiwan's economic growth out of the worldwide recession and into a new era of sophisticated industry and technology. Did such a consensus emerge from the discussion?

THE 1982 CONSENSUS AMONG ECONOMISTS

A joint statement was prepared at the end of the August 18, 1982 economic forum by two leading economists of opposing views, Tso-yung Wang of the National Taiwan University and Sho-chieh Tsiang, Director of the Chung-hua Institution for Economic Research. The two men, each representing a particular viewpoint, although the number of adherents on each side is unknown, presented their common understanding as follows:

On production policy. Inducements of investment should concentrate on production investment which can more rapidly increase productivity inasmuch as economic growth of this type will contribute to economic stability. Since Taiwan's industry relies upon export, strong competitiveness on the world market must be maintained. Maintenance and strengthening of competitiveness require free competition while government control and protection will only reduce competitiveness and hinder the growth of Taiwan's industry. Past vaciilations in controlling exports and imports have therefore been harmful and should be replaced during the next couple of years by an unambiguous and consistent policy which will be credible to the business community.

On fiscal policy. A consistently surplus budget over the previous decades was an important stabilizing force in the Taiwan economy. Since revenue shortages have appeared in recent years, the government should strive to balance the budget. It should eschew budget deficits that would undermine price stability and constitute a source of self-reenforcing inflation. The tax burden, though admittedly not above that in many welfare states, was regarded by both men as high and inequitable. In the interest of a more equitable tax burden and to encourage business expansion, they therefore advocated an expansion of the tax base, a general reduction of the income tax rates, and selective tax exemption and reduction for business enterprises. Both would regard the use of public spending as an appropriate *short-run* measure to stimulate aggregate demand.

On financial policy. While agreeing on the external impact on Taiwan's prices, both men were agreed on the positive correlation between money supply and the price level. They agreed on maintaining the annual increase in money supply at 10 to 15 percent, in order to prevent price inflation, allowance having been made for an increasing demand for money as a result of economic growth and the empirical phenomenon in Taiwan of a changing income elasticity of demand for money. Both agreed on the contribution to economic equilibrium and optimal use of resources of interest and exchange rates that are determined in perfectly competitive markets. Both also agreed, however, that while efforts were being made toward the determination of interest rates by the free market and toward completely flexible exchange rates, the market conditions were as yet unprepared for such total freedom. Hence these are long-term goals to aspire to and, by implication, not realistic short-run objectives. Both ventured to suggest that the depreciation of the New Taiwan dollar during 1982 from NT $36 to NT $40 per U.S. dollar and a prevailing real interest rate of 5 to 6 percent seemed appropriate.

Summing up their statement, the two economists stressed the need for an appropriate social framework most compatible with economic development. To them such a framework would include the establishment of economic law and order and social discipline, a complete overhaul and renovation of the administrative structure, and the establishment of certain necessary modern institutions.

It would be quite unrealistic to expect complete agreement among theoretical economists. The joint statement described above made no mention of what specific industries should be encouraged through tax reductions and exemptions. The two economists did not stake out a common position on the long-term use of government investment in promoting economic growth and, by implication, might not have an agreed position on the relative roles of public versus private enterprise. They offered no common understanding of how one could tell when market forces alone should be allowed to determine the internal and external prices of money. They left essentially vague the precise nature of the modern institutions to be established. Some of the issues are probably technicalities that could not be gone into at a public meeting. Others are equally technical points on which economists, like other members of the public, can be expected to disagree on various grounds—different interpretations of facts, varying subjective judgments, and the like. Yet what is surprising is that there was in fact a vast ground on which the academic economists in Taiwan were apparently in agreement. Even the businessmen who, unlike academicians, have to resolve short-run, if not immediate difficulties, such as a cash flow emergency, were apparently agreed on the long-term objectives of the Taiwan economy.

A FUNDAMENTAL REAL CONSENSUS

A final point stands out clearly from the wide-ranging dialogue on the future of the Taiwan economy we have reviewed. That is, the entire discussion focused on institutional and structural change of the domestic economy. Although protection for some industries may be more than a passing thought in some quarters, there is never any real doubt that Taiwan should continue its development as an open market economy striving to become progressively more involved with the rest of the world. Nor has there been any real dissenting voice on the desirability of enhancing Taiwan's regional and even global role in trade, finance, and transportation as a means of enhancing the island's security. Internationalization is a generally accepted direction; R&D and high-technology industry are expected to spearhead the forward march. This is the real and fundamental consensus Taiwan has reached.

NOTES

1. That is in the years between the end of the 1970s and the beginning of the 1980s.

2. See the report on Chiang's address at the first meeting of the 59th session of the Legislative Yuan (Parliament) on February 25, 1977 in Chen, Kao-tung, ed., *China Yearbook 1978* (Taipei: China Publishing Co., 1978), pp. 688–703.

3. This refers to the ten major infrastructure projects that were then being completed and the additional 12 projects that were to follow.

4. *China Yearbook, 1978*, pp. 703–708.

5. See Chiang Ching-kuo's message to the 60th session of the Legislative Yuan on September 23, 1977. *China Yearbook 1978*, pp. 708–724.

6. See Premier Chiang's report to the first meeting of the 61st session of the Legislative Yuan on February 21, 1978. *China Yearbook 1979*, pp. 695–706.

7. Chiang Kai-shek's unfinished term as President was completed by Yen Chia-kan, who was Chiang's Vice-president. *China Yearbook, 1979*, pp. 731–744.

8. In 1978 the income share of the top 20 percent of all households was 37.2 percent of that of all households; that of the bottom 20 percent was 8.9 percent. In 1964 the corresponding ratios were 41.1 percent and 7.7 percent respectively. Council for Economic Planning and Development, *Social Welfare Indicators, Republic of China* (Taipei: September 1979), p. 9.

9. See the February 20, 1979 report by Premier Sun to the first meeting of the 63rd Legislative Yuan, *China Yearbook 1980*, pp. 646–659.

10. See Premier Sun's address at the first meeting of the 71st session of the Legislative Yuan reported in the *World Journal* (San Francisco), February 28, 1983.

11. *The Commercial Times* (Taipei), October 1, 1982.

12. Address by Y. T. Chao before the Conference on Taiwan industrial development, sponsored by the Institute of Economic Research, Academia Sinica, reprinted in *Industry of Free China* 59, No. 3 (Taipei: Council for Economic Planning and Development, March 1983), pp. 1–6. On point 5 mentioned above, Chao seemed to favor a pyramidal structure of firms in which a large manufacturer (for example, Toyota) would be backstopped by a number of specialized satellite firms as opposed to complete vertical integration in a single firm.

13. Reported in *The Commercial Times*, January 3, 1983.

14. In 1984, following the election of President Chiang Ching-kuo to a second term, Hsü Li-teh became the Economic Affairs Minister in the new Cabinet, succeeding Chao, who took over the chairmanship of the Council for Economic Planning and Development. Hsü's former Vice-minister took over the Treasury portfolio. Hence the same ideas are expected to wield essentially the same influence as before.

15. In real terms, the annual increase over the preceding year of Taiwan's gross capital formation varied from 13 to over 15 percent in 1978-80. In 1981 the rate dropped to 3 percent; it fell to minus 2 percent in 1982. This depressed state of investment compares with comparable low annual rates of increase in 1976 and 1977. See *National Income of the Republic of China, 1951-82* (Taipei: Directorate-General of Budget, Accounting and Statistics, December 1982), p. 12.

16. *The Commercial Times*, January 1, 1983.

17. Ibid., January 2, 1983.

18. The views expressed by Ku Cheng-fu are echoed by many others. See, for instance, the views of Hsu You-hsiang, head of Far Eastern Textiles, *The Commercial Times*, January 1, 1983.

19. According to Chen Chao-nan, during 1973-81, the real interest rate from the business borrower's point of view was 2-3 percent a year. This was based on a peak annual nominal interest rate of no more than 14 percent and a wholesale price index of 11.5 percent. *The Commercial Times* Forum, August 16, 1982.

3

INWARD TRANSFER AND INTERNAL GROWTH OF KNOWLEDGE-INTENSIVE INDUSTRIES

INTRODUCTION

Having concluded as a matter of principle that the Taiwan economy must undergo structural adjustment in favor of the knowledge-intensive industries, and simultaneously increase its overall productive capacity, the ROC authorities have since 1979 progressively built up the momentum in their search for appropriate answers to some of the relevant questions. It is still too early to assess the net effect of all the measures adopted so far although some of the policies have already begun to bear fruit. Since the improvements desired in the production function through innovation and adjustment will include changes in management, business organization, and even other institutions, the term "knowledge-intensive industry" is used in lieu of "technology-intensive industry," so as to preclude any unduly restrictive interpretation of the word "technology."

If new knowledge-intensive businesses are to be established in Taiwan without undue delay, they must be promoted either by domestic entrepreneurs who already possess such capability or by qualified foreign entrepreneurs. What inducements can and should be offered to accelerate this process? What has already been done?

Second, in the longer run, the expansion of knowledge-intensive investments will be aided by acquisition of new knowledge through public and private investment in R&D. Again, there is the same incentive question.

Third, a two-fold question of priority in resource allocation follows: What specific kinds of industries should be considered "knowledge-intensive" and of these what particular branches should be given preference in granting special inducements?

Fourth, new knowledge is either "embodied" in machinery or equipment or, in a sense, "embodied" in talented *and* experienced scientists, engineers, technicians, managers, planners, and administrators. A piece of sophisticated equipment will sometimes require highly trained engineers and technicians to assure its proper function. Experienced managers are needed for complex operations. When new knowledge is acquired through licensing, the seemingly disembodied information may require additional "know-how" as a joint input, which is often tantamount to knowledge embodied in labor. Accordingly, a separate series of questions for Taiwan has to do with the means of obtaining the service of three categories of such qualified persons: nonethnic Chinese foreign nationals, ethnic Chinese residing outside Taiwan, and present and future recruits in Taiwan.

Fifth, once a knowledge-intensive innovation or adjustment has been successfully developed or introduced from abroad, how can it be most expeditiously disseminated and widely applied? "Sharing" is only one aspect of knowledge interchange, which can have a stimulative and creative effect of its own on the development of inventions. What measures can be devised to produce a greater impact in this direction?

The following account will show that attempts have been made to *answer* the preceding questions by Taiwan's policy makers—some completely and quite firmly, others only partially or more tentatively. None, however, has been totally ignored. As one might expect, all the issues calling for attention have not emerged at the same time. Hence awareness of their seriousness or urgency has varied. Above all, change has probably been slowest to come by only when certain age-old institutions and attitudes are involved.

Finally, even as the policies addressing the above questions are still being developed, R&D work in a number of economic sectors has been going on and its results have been applied in production. It would be a serious mistake to regard the present emphasis on knowledge-intensive industry, which is an overall adjustment of the economic structure, as evidence that there has been no such industry until now or, worse still, that there has been no such awareness before. Quite to the contrary, the agricultural sector, which has been overtaken by the more rapidly advancing industries, including the attention-catching and glamorous silicon chip and integrated circuit, has for some time been focusing considerable attention on new knowledge and the R&D effort producing such knowledge. Equally significant is the lesson one can learn from Taiwan's successful application of R&D outside the industrial sector.

INCREASING THE PROFITABILITY OF NEW INVESTMENT

The ROC authorities have chosen to encourage investment in knowledge-intensive industries primarily by enhancing its profitability and by reducing the risk the investors must bear. The inducements are greatest in the case of enterprises located in the Hsin-chu Science-based Industrial Park (H.S.I.P.) which has been established in the present big push for high technology. Legislation setting up the H.S.I.P. in July 1979[1] has the effect of enhancing profits for the approved investor in the following manner:

1. *Tax exemption.* Central to this approach is an income tax holiday for five consecutive years, the investor being allowed to elect any of the first five years as the initial year. Such an approved S.I.P. enterprise is also exempted from the business tax and the commodity tax—completely if the goods produced are for export or partially if the goods manufactured are for sale on the domestic market. A similar distinction is made in exemption from the import tariff between finished products exported and those sold domestically.
2. *Tax ceiling.* Park enterprises enjoy a 22 percent ceiling in the income tax they pay. In contrast, other businesses pay a maximum income tax of 25 percent even under the special legislation encouraging investment first adopted in 1960 as amended.[2]
3. *Tax credit for stockholders.* If a Park enterprise reinvests its undistributed earnings in the enterprise, the amount can be treated as a credit against the stockholder's consolidated income. This is intended to encourage the latter to reinvest for enterprise growth.
4. *Reduction of land rent.* The governing body of the Park (S.I.P.) Administration (S.I.P.A.) may reduce or even completely forgive the land rent payable by a Park enterprise if the latter's technology is regarded by the S.I.P.A. as especially desirable.

The government further tries to increase the potential return to the private investor and reduce his risk by offering to contribute to the original investment without encroaching on private control. The following measures serve this purpose:

The National Science Council, which is the superior government agency overseeing the S.I.P.A., may, together with two government-designated financial institutions and at the request of the private investor, invest up to 49 percent of the capital of a Park enterprise. Furthermore, patents and know-how could be counted as high as 25 percent of total equity. It is conceivable, therefore, for an investor to contribute financially no more than 26 percent of his own capital in order to start up an enterprise in the Hsin-chu S.I.P.

Additional low-cost loans are also available.

Not to be discounted are the inherent advantages of the industrial park concept and some special circumstances adding to the locational advantage of Hsin-chu. By gathering many high-technology enterprises at one place, certain advantages derived from external economies may be magnified for all the individual enterprises, for example, availability of a highly trained labor pool; repair, maintenance, marketing, consulting, and other services that will develop of their own accord; the services which S.I.P.A. provides directly. There are other special favorable circumstances which would not be available elsewhere and which have made Hsin-chu the choice location. That is, Hsin-chu is the home of the Tsinghua and Chiaotung Universities, two of Taiwan's best educational institutions in science and technology. The intended linkage between science and industry and between education and employment is obvious. Finally, inside H.S.I.P. is located Taiwan's Industrial Technology Institute which had in 1983 separate research laboratories for electronics, energy, industrial materials, mining, and mechanics. A separate food industry research institute, established before the H.S.I.P., is located outside the Park in Hsin-chu.

EMBODIED KNOWLEDGE AND THE HUMAN RESOURCE

The demand for new knowledge embodied in the human resource implies a demand for sophisticated and experienced persons of skills and talents. In Taiwan this manpower requirement used to be interpreted narrowly as a demand for physical scientists and engineers.

More recently, the scope has been broadened to include, in expanding concentric circles, management personnel, social scientists, and administrators.[3] Specialists in the life sciences and such hybridized fields as biochemistry and biophysics have also been included.

The only two ways for a country to augment its human capital, as is the case with physical capital assets, are importation and domestic capital formation through investment in education, training, and R&D personnel and facilities. A special situation is the presence in countries outside Taiwan of a large pool of highly educated ethnic Chinese whose talents and experience are among those in demand. This pool has been accumulated over several decades from students and others originating from both Taiwan and Chinese communities elsewhere in the world. A few figures will illustrate the size of this pool and the order of magnitude of the present demand for human capital.

According to a survey cited in a report on an ROC plan to "strengthen the education, training and recruitment of high-level science and technology personnel," in March 1983, the demand and supply of such personnel over a two-year period in terms of M.A. and Ph.D. degree holders are as follows:

TABLE 3.1. Demand and Supply of High-Level Science and Technology Personnel

		Pure Science	Engineering Mechanical	Electrical	Civil	Chemical	Total
Demand by private industry and the public sector	M.A.	165	963	958	177	143	2,406
	Ph.D.	102	241	292	67	60	762
Supply	M.A.	493	673	673	220	252	2,311
	Ph.D.	17	6	31	12	11	77
Surplus (+) or deficit (−)	M.A.	+328	−290	−285	+43	+109	−95
	Ph.D.	−85	−235	−261	−55	−49	−685

Source: Wei Yung, *A National Plan for Strengthening the Education, Training and Recruitment of High-Level Science and Technology Personnel, A Summarized Report*, April 4, 1983.

On the other hand, between 1949 and 1980 inclusive, 63,061 persons left Taiwan on student visas for advanced studies abroad. Other ethnic Chinese in advanced studies during this period who originated from other areas or left Taiwan in other capacities are not included in this figure. Of the 63,000 only a small proportion actually returned to Taiwan.[4] Many of the remainder would not qualify on the supply side by field of study, age, experience and current and recent occupation. Nevertheless these rough estimates which probably consist of an underestimated demand and a potentially much smaller supply than the gross figures shown here suggest that the external pool mentioned earlier may well constitute a source of human capital from which imports can be derived.

Some of the ethnic Chinese talents, that is, human capital, to be imported would be destined for employment with private employers or in government agencies. Such employment could be either on a long-term basis or for short periods only. Nonethnic Chinese talents presumably can also be induced to go to Taiwan and many have done so, as visiting scientists, engineers, professors, and so on. Both Chinese and others can probably be induced to work in Taiwan on a longer term or even permanent basis as self-employed entrepreneurs. The offer of assistance in funding to establish an enterprise in the Hsin-chu S.I.P. is apparently conceived in the same manner.

There are certain civil service requirements, originally established to limit political interference with hiring and to give protection in opportunities for promotion and tenure to members of the civil service, that now bar qualified professionals without the requisite civil service credentials from civil service positions and sufficiently attractive salary levels. Legislation to reform these rules promises to be a time-consuming process so that stop gap measures must be devised in the near term. Nevertheless salary scale adjustments on a long-term basis are a major plank of the government's program to recruit upper level personnel to staff a knowledge-intensive economy and a correspondingly sophisticated public sector and government administration as its support and complement. In fact, it is a merit of the ROC government to have recognized the need for increasing sophistication in the government itself as the private sector leaves behind certain LDC characteristics. Other measures designed to upgrade and train currently employed persons include in-service training and interchange of personnel among government, industry, and educational institutions. For recruiting high-level personnel working in an H.S.I.P.

enterprise, special housing and other facilities for schooling, shopping, and so on have been provided. These all aim at improving the investment climate for the recruitment, retention, and accumulation of human capital in Taiwan.

Finally, it should be mentioned that the effort to recruit scientists and technologists and other sophisticated talents from Taiwan is not new. The Commission of Assistance to Young Chinese in the Executive Yuan and the National Science Council have been active in such work for a number of years. But the ratio of returnees to the number of students who left Taiwan for advanced studies abroad was only about 11 percent in three decades (1949-80), not counting some 3,200 persons recruited by the National Science Council during the later years in the same period, mostly for short terms.[5]

In the medium term and long run, the demand for highly sophisticated human capital must rely on an expansion of supply. This can happen only through an expansion of R&D expenditure and of training institutions and personnel. Underlying such developments will have to be thorough readjustment of Taiwan's educational institutions and policies and their closer integration with the country's economic development. The 1983 plan of education, training, and recruitment of science and technology personnel promises to be the beginning of such a program, but it still is just a beginning.

INDUSTRY AND R&D PRIORITIES

The high-technology enterprises which the Hsin-chu S.I.P. wishes to attract must satisfy a number of criteria. First, in addition to manufacturing (except of course for consulting concerns), they must have engineering, design, and development activities. Second, their work must be free from environmental pollution. These preliminary conditions apart, preference is given to certain specific industries. This industry list, subject to change from time to time, is compiled by S.I.P.A. As of 1983 the list included electronics and information, precision instrument and machinery, high technology materials, energy science, aeronautical engineering, and biological engineering.[6]

It appears that this list of high technology industries is essentially a subset of the larger group of key or what the ROC government has described as "strategic" industries. These industries are selected especially to give Taiwan new comparative advantage on the world market, especially in light of the growth of lower priced labor-intensive exports from Taiwan's competitors; to provide more higher value-added products, including many that are knowledge-intensive, so as to accelerate the rate of economic growth; and to act as a catalyst of growth through both demonstration and linkage.

Two principal ideas underlie the selection of these criteria and of special industries. On the one hand, Taiwan's security requirements are reflected in the criteria of choice. For example, the development of an independent productive capacity for defense needs is one. The gradual development of a more complete, mutually supporting, productive structure of intermediate products is another. This is why enterprises producing and doing R&D on materials for sophisticated products are encouraged.

On the other hand, Taiwan's special situation as an island economy with limited space and natural resources has dictated some of the constraints. Polluting activities are discouraged; high energy users are not welcome.[7] In the case of S.I.P. enterprises, the limited space in the Park would further rule out large-scale, space-using enterprises.[8] The need for minimizing vulnerability to external trade fluctuation, as mentioned in the previous chapter, apparently has already lowered the earlier emphasis on capital-intensive industries with large fixed assets that are of limited specific use, unless they possess other redeeming characteristics.[9] Since the nature of new enterprises depends ultimately on the decision of private entrepreneurs—the government is neither willing nor able to do everything the private sector fails to do—the list of industries to be given special preference either inside the Park or in Taiwan as a whole will be reviewed periodically.

Some recent public discussion has drawn attention to additional economic considerations in expanding knowledge-intensive industries. The latter include consideration of timing according to the relevant product life cycle. That is, for success in competing with foreign producers, Taiwan is likely to do better if its new entries on the world market are goods whose current exporters are losing their comparative advantage precisely as Taiwan gains hers.[10] This implies a close watch on R&D and industrial developments in countries that are now ahead of Taiwan in industrial and technological sophistication.

Regarding R&D priorities, if certain enterprises are to be encouraged, the corresponding industry-specific R&D needs to be emphasized. The ROC government has offered to provide guidance for the private sector looking for the appropriate direction of spending on R&D. The eight priority fields announced in January 1983[11] were (1) energy, (2) sophisticated materials for industry, (3) information, (4) automation, (5) bio-engineering, (6) laser technology, (7) prevention and cure of hepatitis, and (8) food technology. The same priority is applicable to the recruitment, education, and training of knowledge-intensive science and technology personnel that the March 1983 S&T manpower program tries to implement.

Reverse linkage—from a specific R&D target to the encouragement of investments for manufacturing selected products—has also taken place. For example, in order to promote industrial automation, 51 specific items have already been selected as targets for encouragement through loans on preferred terms.[12]

A RECAPITULATION OF THE 1983 GOVERNMENT PROGRAM TO PROMOTE SCIENCE AND TECHNOLOGY

For an overview of the ROC government's plan to promote knowledge-intensive industries, its S&T program for 1983 can be summarized as follows:

1. *Expansion of R&D expenditure.* A general expansion in this category by all public and private enterprises is to be accompanied by the establishment of special funds and research foundations to be sponsored by private business and labor unions.
2. *An intensified program to educate, train, and recruit sophisticated S&T talents.* The March 1983 national program described earlier falls into this category. A flurry of investment and S&T seminars held abroad by MOEA and SIPA personnel in 1983 was a visible portion of this substantial effort. Faculty recruitment from abroad for institutions of higher learning in Taiwan, a long established practice, has been stepped up. A greatly expanded graduate training and fellowship program for advanced work or in-service training and interchange among government, industry, and academic institutions is envisaged. Institutional adjustments among existing academic institutions are promised but this is likely to lag because of tradition and vested interests.
3. *Promotion of H.S.I.P activities.* This is probably among the most active—and incidentally most visible—parts of the entire effort. In addition to the formulation of policy guidelines described above,

the S.I.P.A. has made special efforts to simplify and shorten administrative procedures and to provide service for Park enterprises and residents.
4. *Provision of financial and tax incentives and simplification of export-import procedures for Park enterprises.*
5. *Establishment of a cooperative research and appraisal system.*
6. *Acceleration and expansion of international technology transfer.* This is inseparable from items (2) and (3). Particularly noteworthy is the aspect of technology export by Taiwan. The novel aspect, however, has to do with efforts to expand the consulting service industry in Taiwan and to develop international cooperative activities with a wider group of European countries with which Taiwan has no diplomatic relations.[13]
7. *Expansion of equipment*, library collections, data banks, international sources of information and references on international standards, industrial safety, and so on at the National Science Council and in selected centers.

Item 5 appeared to be just starting in 1983; this is perhaps especially true in its domestic aspect. As mentioned before, revamping educational institutions may prove most time-consuming. For higher level personnel the problem of recruitment has so far taken the form mostly of recruitment from abroad. The recruitment of both entrepreneurs and S&T personnel has become the focus of all efforts at this stage of Taiwan's policy to make technology the motive power of accelerated economic growth.

A PRELIMINARY REVIEW OF THE RECORD

As we have pointed out, the policy described above has not yet been implemented in its entirety. Some aspects, however, have already registered a measure of success. The following account will attempt to present a few illustrative cases from which one can obtain a qualitative impression of the kind of developments afoot.

First, during a period of three and a quarter years, between September 1979 and December 1982, 42 firms were approved for business in the Hsin-chu S.I.P. Two of these later withdrew; two others decided to relocate themselves outside the Park. Of the remaining 38,[14] 29 firms were in operation as of 1982 year-end; the other nine were expected to begin operation soon. The annual net additions of firms so far were: 1979, four; 1980, eight; 1981, 15; 1982, 11. These figures have fallen behind the annual target of 15 new firms for a period of ten years, but not by a large margin for 1981 and 1982.

The 38 firms represent a total investment (including presumably contributions of technology and know-how) valued at NT $2,480 million (approximately US $37 million), which compares with average annual total external investment approvals of US $338 million for 1981-82. All but one of the firms have investments below NT $150 million (US $3.75 million).

Fifty-six percent of the total capital invested in the first 38 firms is represented by wholly Chinese-owned enterprises; wholly U.S.-owned businesses account for 11 percent. The remaining 33 percent of the total investment is represented by joint enterprises involving Chinese, American, British, Singaporean, and Hong Kong owners.

Of the 38 wholly Chinese-owned firms, 26 are in electronics and the information industry; ten are producers of precision equipment and machinery; two are manufacturers of materials supplying high technology industrial users. (The four that have moved out of the Park or have withdrawn are also electronics firms.)

Second, a review of the many topics under study in some of the laboratories of the Industrial Technology Research Institute indicates that they are mostly concerned with cost reduction, new products, search for new types of inputs and resources, and introduction of new technologies. Computer-aided design and manufacturing and software development for VLSI (very large-scale integrated circuits) have occupied a great deal of attention. Robot development has been pushed by specialist teams drawn from various government agencies and engineering schools.

EXAMPLES FROM AGRICULTURAL R&D[15]

Finally, while the effort to develop knowledge-intensive industries in the nonagricultural sector has been the focus of publicity in Taiwan, agricultural R&D has been quietly going on. More accurately, R&D in fishery and fruit planting, especially in agricultural genetics, offers several most interesting examples of how new resources, untapped before, have been made possible through technological advances.

The first two examples illustrate how a vertical dimension has been introduced in resource use. That is to say, if we think of crop cultivation as the use of land in a two-dimensional space, use of land on a mountain, or raising fish in inland ponds, water reservoirs and coastal waters introduces a third dimension.

Taiwan has grown temperate zone fruits (pears and apples) on land at higher elevations. Two pear varieties are commonly cultivated in Taiwan. One is the so-called plains pear which is derived from *Pyrus serotina*. ("Hengshan-li" is the leading variety of this group.) All of the plains pears need less chilling and thus are commonly cultivated on plains and hilly lands of 500 meters or less above sea-level. The other is a temperate zone pear originated from *Pyrus bretschneideri* or other species. ("New Century," "Twentieth Century," and so on are popular varieties of this group in Taiwan.) The temperate zone pears have a relatively long period of dormancy in which they need long hours of low temperature in winter to meet their psysiological requirements. Hence, varieties of this kind must be cultivated in areas as high as 1,700 meters above sea level in Taiwan.

In order to reduce transportation cost and to minimize soil erosion through top-working, the dormancy-terminated twig of such varieties as "New Century" growing in high mountain areas can be pruned and top-worked onto the plains pear "Hengshan-li" in early spring to yield fruits of both varieties. In the beginning of this effort the effect of the grafting lasted one season only. Further research has since increased the length of time to three years.

Coastal aquaculture (raising fish and shellfish in coastal waters) in Taiwan has been mainly limited to the intertidal zone. The cultivated area totaled 16,229 ha. with a production of 31,000 M.T. in 1981. According to Council for Agricultural Planning and Development (CAPD) specialists, it could be expanded to about 125,000 ha. if the waters within a 20-meter depth were fully utilized. Using currently available technology, it is estimated that by the end of this decade, the cultivated area of coastal waters will be tripled to about 45,000 ha., with a total production of 90,000 M.T.

Trap-net fishery is another way of exploiting the natural fishery resources in coastal waters. Through technological improvements, the third generation trap-nets, which were originally imported from Japan, can efficiently operate to catch fish from different water levels within a 100-meter depth. CAPD estimates suggest that the number of trap-nets will increase from 19 sets in 1981 to 200 sets by the end of the 1980s, with the catch rising from 3,000 M.T. to 30,000 M.T. during the period.

Introducing the Time Dimension

A different approach in agricultural R&D can be illustrated by work on watermelon through the application of horticultural techniques and plant regulators, which control the plant's growth process lest production be concentrated in a particular period of the year. Such horticultural crops as watermelon, carambola and guava, for example, can now be harvested in Taiwan monthly. Other fruits such as grape, pear, wax jambo (wax apple), sweet sop (sugar apple), and Indian jujube can also be successfully harvested more than once a year. This evens out price and output fluctuations and increases the total income of growers.

Increasing Production and Value-Added

In the production of a highly popular fish (tilapia fry), the technique of hybridization has been used to produce all-male fingerlings. By stocking these fingerlings in ponds, undesirable reproduction can be eliminated. This method has been widely applied since 1970, resulting in a drastic increase of tilapia production—from 34,781 M.T. in 1980 to 48,481 M.T. in 1981.

These examples serve to remind us not only that the potential R&D efforts are by no means limited to the nonagricultural sector but that results are not gained overnight. Taiwan's R&D workers in agriculture (understood in the broad sense) have had a long row to hoe. The same can be said of the present drive to develop high technology industries.

NOTES

1. For an overview of S&T development and R&D policy in Taiwan the reader should consult K. T. Li, *My Views on Taiwan's Economic Development* (Taipei: n.p., August 1980), and Li's address before the Chinese National Association of Industry and Commerce in Taipei on August 27, 1981, and that at the Sixth Joint Conference of the U.S.-ROC and ROC-U.S. Economic Councils on November 9, 1981. The program for the development of science and technology was first adopted by the Executive Yuan on May 17, 1979, and has been updated periodically.

2. The law offers special tax incentives to investments in "strategic industries" which have been identified in considerable detail in terms of specific commodities.

3. See Wei Yung, *"Jen-ts'ai Yün-yung yü Kuo-chia Chien-she"* [On the Recruitment of Talented Persons for Nation-Building], address before the annual Chinese-American Meeting on Science and Technology, Seattle, May 21, 1983.

4. Between 1950 and 1980, inclusive, the number of students who returned to Taiwan totalled 7,240 or 11.5 percent. For the same period, the proportion in the S&T category was 11.1 percent (3,932 returnees compared to 35,359 students who left). The proportion fluctuated considerably from year to year, reaching as high as 31.6 percent in 1976 for all categories. Reported by Yao Shun, *"Tang-ch'ien Wo-kuo K'o-chi Fa-chan yü Jen't'sai P'ei-yü"* [The Current State of S&T Personnel and Development in the ROC], (Taipei: N.p., October 1981.)

5. See Note 4.

6. See Paul C. Y. Chu, "The Science-based Industrial Park" in *Republic of China Investment Seminar* (Republic of China: Ministry of Economic Affairs), presentation in Los Angeles, Dallas, New York, Boston, Chicago and San Francisco, June 1–15, 1983.

7. The MOEA (Ministry of Economic Affairs) declared in Summer 1983 that it would no longer issue permits for such enterprises as new cement plants.

8. Conceivably, an enterprise started within the Park may have to move out later when it outgrows its "living space."

9. Selected chemical industries and the automotive industry probably belong to the last category.

10. Hsiao Feng-hsiung, "Ko-chi Fa-chan So Ying K'ou-lü chih Ching-chi Yin-su" [Economic Considerations in the Development of S&T] in *The Commercial Times* (Taipei), April 5, 1982.

11. *The Commercial Times*, January 2, 1983.

12. Ibid., July 25, 1982.

13. For example, West Germany.

14. Four more were approved as of April 1983. Reports of the H.S.I.P.A., various dates.

15. The following are based on interviews with specialists in the Council of Agricultural Policy and Development in January 1983.

4

INSTITUTIONAL DEVELOPMENT AND THE MOBILIZATION OF CAPITAL

A DUAL TASK IN CHANNELING SAVINGS TO INVESTMENT

In the 1980s the continuation of economic growth in Taiwan is no longer constrained by insufficient savings as it was in the 1950s or as it still is in many LDCs today.[1] Rather a prerequisite of continuing development is to mobilize the society's large flow of savings in such a manner that they can be used to best advantage from the point of view of both economic growth and the distribution of its benefits. The accomplishment of this dual task requires inter alia[2] that available savings as a whole be channelled to investments *primarily* according to their productivity and that individual savers can enjoy equal access to the markets of alternative instruments of financial assets.

To say that the allocation of savings be based *primarily* on the relative productivity or profitability of investments is to allow for the fact that political and security considerations will always play a role in the real world in allocating resources, including their use in long-term investments. Moreover, apart from this qualification, investing in new projects in general and in what people in Taiwan call "strategic industries" is not without substantial risk. If estimates of risk by private businessmen, based on their more limited information and financial resources than those available to the government, exceed those of the public authorities, and/or if the business community's propensity for risk taking is lower, special efforts would have to be made, probably through government intervention, to channel more savings into certain favored industries than otherwise might be automatically invested. Hence optimal economic policy implementation would require that the favored sectors of the economy be adequately provided with investible funds. At the same time, that the same sectors will not be over-supplied with funds at a greater potential distortion of the economic structure and cost to the other sectors than should be risked also merits serious consideration.

From the point of view of the savers, if the investments funded by their savings turn out to be at least as profitable as they have planned, it is important that they enjoy equal access to the available financial instruments and that they be free to choose from among these assets. In addition, it is conducive to such a development if the types of financial assets bearing different characteristics in terms of return, risk, availability, and convenience, are multiplied because individual savers who do not value these qualities equally will then have a wider range of assets to select. In particular, although the rate of return is only one of the characteristics of financial assets, their yield, especially as a result of capital gains, can significantly influence income distribution. Hence the savers' access to assets of potentially high profitability is of major significance.

CHARACTERISTICS OF TAIWAN'S FINANCIAL MARKETS AND BUSINESS BEHAVIOR

The extent to which savers in Taiwan can freely choose from financial assets of varying yields and risks is greatly affected by the major role of the banking system acting as intermediaries between savers and investors. Understanding of this issue is facilitated by a quick review of some of the principal characteristics of the behavioral patterns of Taiwan's savers, businessmen, and financial institutions.

First, households in Taiwan, including nonprofit organizations, are the most important single source of savings. In 1980, for instance, when gross national savings amounted to NT $481 billion, or 33.2 percent of GNP at current prices, the household sector was responsible for 38.2 percent of the total. This compares with 36.9 percent of total savings derived from the private and public business sectors together—5.6 percent from private enterprises, 7.5 percent from government enterprises and 23.8 percent from depreciation reserves. During the two decades since 1965 the remainder was accounted for by government institutions. The share of households in total gross savings stayed at around 40 percent, falling slightly only during recession.[3]

Second, among the financial assets held by the household savers, deposits with financial intermediaries such as banks, trust companies, and so on, far exceed holdings of stocks, bonds, and other instruments, selection of which involves a more direct evaluation of business prospects and risks by the savers themselves. This can be seen from figures in Table 4.1 from 1965 and 1979. Between 1965 and 1979 there was a substantial increase in the proportion of funds placed with financial intermediaries, principally banks. A larger share of the corporate stocks held by the household sector was probably in

TABLE 4.1. Percent Distribution of Financial Assets Held by Households and Non-profit Organizations

	1965 NT$ million	1965 Percent	1979 NT$ million	1979 Percent
1. Currency and demand deposits	10,870	16.02	141,061	10.52
2. Time and savings deposits and foreign currency deposits	21,576	31.81	447,302	33.35
3. Trust funds	–	–	47,701	3.56
4. Reserves of insurance companies	627	0.92	26,659	1.99
2, 3 & 4 Subtotal	22,203	32.73	662,723	38.90
5. Commercial papers, bankers' acceptance, government and corporate bonds	437	0.64	9,253	0.69
6. Corporate stocks	20,927	30.86	396,342	29.55
5 & 6 Subtotal	21,364	31.50	405,595	30.24
7. Shares of noncorporate business receivables from and deposits with firms	12,341	18.19	250,514	18.68
8. Other domestic assets	1,060	1.56	22,296	1.66
Total	67,838	100.00	1,341,128	100.00

Source: Chiu, P. "Performance of Financial Institutions in Taiwan," p. 434.

the hands of the nonprofit organizations rather than the individual households. Some of the loans made to, and deposits with, some firms not in the form of regular commercial papers also border on deposits with financial intermediaries. Hence the role of intermediaries is even larger than the figures in Table 4.1 indicate.

Third, businessmen in Taiwan, like their counterparts in Japan, use bank loans to raise medium- and long-term funds. In his highly informative work on Taiwan's financial institutions, Paul Chiu referred to the average ratio of equity to total assets of private manufacturing business in Taiwan in 1976-79—38.55 percent—as much higher than the corresponding ratio of 17.5 percent for major enterprises in Japan in 1975.[4] Nevertheless the ratio had fallen from 40.2 percent in 1971-75. Besides, if one were to look at the ratio of a narrower aggregate of (1) "loans from financial institutions" and (2) loans from other private enterprises and households to total assets of the same manufacturing business,[5] the increase in dependence on the domestic banking intermediaries for medium- and longer-term loans in recent years might actually be greater. The ratio of this narrower loan aggregate to total assets in Taiwan's manufacturing business rose from 30.04 percent in 1971-75 to 33.70 percent in 1976-79.

Fourth, the locally incorporated commercial banks are the most important source of both short- and long-term financing in Taiwan. Their share in the total financial assets (in year-end figures) owned by the principal institutions of Taiwan's organized financial market averaged 52.91 percent in 1976-80. Together with the branch banks of foreign institutions in Taipei, the domestic and foreign commercial banks were responsible during this period for an average of 56.87 percent.[6]

Tables 4.2 and 4.3 reveal two characteristics of the commercial banks and of all financial institutions including the investment trusts and insurance companies: First, between 1965 and 1982 the magnitude of their respective investments in securities (bonds and stocks) rose much faster than that of loans and discounts. Second, while the share of the private sector of the economy increased significantly in total investments in securities, its share in short-term loans and discounts fell—especially between 1973 and 1982, that is, after the first oil crisis. As we shall see, these developments seem to reflect both institutional changes as a result of deliberate policy and the practice of the commercial banks in short-term lending.

TABLE 4.2. Selected Assets of all Financial Institutions (NT$ million)

INDEX

Year end	Investment in Securities	Loans and Discounts
1965	100.0	100.0
1973	308.5	569.0
1982	4,794.6	3,584.4

VALUES AND PERCENT DISTRIBUTIONS

	Total Value	Percent	Government Value	Percent	Government Enterprises Value	Percent	Financial Institutions Value	Percent	Private Enterprises Value	Percent
					Investment in Securities					
Year end										
1965	4,537	100.0	2,271	50.0	1,243	27.4	143	3.2	880	19.4
1973	13,997	100.0	6,646	47.5	2,536	18.1	476	3.4	4,339	31.0
1982	217,533	100.0	37,061	17.0	42,609	19.6	23,055	10.6	114,808	52.8
					Loans and Discounts (Nonfinancial institutions only)					
1965	37,660	100.0	5,235	13.9	5,717	15.2	—		26,717	70.9
1973	214,350	100.0	8,059	3.8	22,719	10.6	—		183,572	85.6
1982	1,350,225	100.0	44,972	3.3	259,915	19.3	—		1,045,338	77.4

Source: *A Supplement to Financial Statistics Monthly*, Taiwan District, *Republic of China Monthly* (Taipei: The Central Bank of China, Economic Research Dept., Oct. 1983), pp. 353–381.

TABLE 4.3. Selected Assets of all Deposit Money Banks (NT$ million)

INDEX

Year end	Investment in Securities	Loans and Discounts
1965	100.0	100.0
1973	248.9	582.4
1982	4,689.0	3,825.3

VALUES AND PERCENT DISTRIBUTIONS

Year end	Total Value	Total Percent	Government Value	Government Percent	Government Enterprises Value	Government Enterprises Percent	Financial Institutions Value	Financial Institutions Percent	Private Enterprises Value	Private Enterprises Percent
					Investment in Securities					
1965	3,516	100.0	1,889	53.7	941	26.8	143	4.1	543	15.4
1973	8,754	100.0	4,527	51.7	2,285	26.1	465	5.3	1,477	16.9
1982	164,867	100.0	33,024	20.0	21,894	13.3	18,736	11.4	91,213	55.3
					Loans and Discounts (Nonbanks only)					
1965	33,203	100.0	1,764	5.3	5,717	17.2	—	—	25,722	77.5
1973	193,385	100.0	3,573	1.8	22,719	11.7	—	—	167,093	86.4
1982	1,270,132	100.0	35,996	2.8	259,880	20.4	—	—	974,256	72.8

Source: A Supplement to Financial Statistics Monthly, Taiwan District, *Republic of China Monthly* (Taipei: The Central Bank of China, Economic Research Dept., Oct. 1983), pp. 69–94.

A QUESTION OF EQUAL ACCESS TO THE CAPITAL MARKET

Given the pivotal role of banks as the principal intermediary between savers and business investors, their lending policy exerts considerable influence on resource allocation and the direction of national development. Two questions come to the fore. First, do some economic sectors and/or types of business face unequal access to the supply of funds? Second, will the policy to promote selected strategic industries be complemented by a proportionate flow of capital?

It appears that the financial authorities periodically have felt that certain economic activities and types of business might not enjoy full access to the capital market. Their customary response on such occasions has been the establishment of specialized lending facilities. The Bank of Communications[7] was made a development bank in January 1979, specializing in extending medium and long-term development credit to industries, investing directly in development projects, offering consultant service on financing, and engaging in such related activities as underwriting, warehousing, and foreign exchange operations. The Farmers Bank of China,[8] originally established on the mainland, specializes in providing credit accommodations to farming, fishing and related rural economic undertakings. Other specialized banks set up several decades ago include the Land Bank of Taiwan (1946), the Cooperative Bank of Taiwan (1946), the Central Trust of China (of mainland China origin), and the Directorate General of Postal Remittance (1962).[9] The Cooperative Bank is a lender and supervisor of the urban cooperatives and the credit departments of farmers' associations and fishermen's associations. The Medium and Small Business Bank of Taiwan was established in mid-1976; seven county banks of the same type were established in 1978-79.[10] Finally, the Export-Import Bank of China was inaugurated in January 1979 and deals with export/import credit, loan guarantees, and so on.

Following their establishment, most of these specialized lending agencies have actually expanded their activities into general commercial banking. Prima facie, one might assume that the special uses of credit for which they were originally established have been more than fulfilled. Yet there are several counter-indications.

First, special lending facilities and task forces were set up by the Central Bank and by the Ministries of Finance and Economic Affairs in 1975-76.[11] The first measure was meant to provide special assistance to the agriculture sector; the second was in response to the aftermath of the 1973-74 oil crisis.

Second, as of March 1, 1983, the deposits of the Postal Savings System, which until then had been redeposited with the Central Bank and partly, therefore, had served to contract the supply of money, were instead placed with the Bank of Communications, the Land Bank, and the Small and Medium Business Bank, respectively. This change was carried out obviously because these institutions were in need of more loanable funds and in order that the borrowers they should serve should receive more capital.

In the third place, with the announced program to speed up development in the high-tech related areas, a Development Fund was set up under the Executive Yuan in 1973. The purposes of the Fund are to invest directly in important productive investments which private business cannot afford or will not undertake, to participate in private investments in technology-intensive and other important investments, to make loans for the same purposes, and to assist in the promotion and transfer to Taiwan of new technology.[12] Financing for this fund came initially from the sale of government-owned stock in the Bank of China and was thus interestingly a reflection of denationalization in the financial sector. It has since absorbed the balances of other special lending facilities and seems to be on the way to becoming an integrated source of development financing. The need for such a special fund to play a catalytic, risk-sharing role in the promotion of selected industries and activities for which private calculations of gain and loss may offer insufficient inducement again indicates the existence of inadequacies in the present capital market. This possibility exists over and above the fact that prospective social gains from the promotion of high tech and other strategic industries external to the undertaking of private investors provides another rationale for the special encouragement of certain industries.

Finally, students of Taiwan's financial markets have pointed to the existence of a sizable "unorganized" or "curb" market where household and perhaps even business savings are supplied to borrowers unable to obtain funds from the regular banks and other lawful financial intermediaries at higher interest rates than are usually charged by banks. This phenomenon exists because, according to some, the borrowers in question do not possess the kind of collateral demanded by the banks. This happens especially when the borrower is a small private businessman. Large enterprises are favored by loan officers in the banks over small ones and public over private enterprises. The loan officers tend to be over-cautious partly because the government is a part-owner of most domestic Taiwan institutions in commercial banking and a bad debt tends to be interpreted by the Supervisory Yuan (a watchdog institution of equal standing to the Executive and the Legislature) as loss of a state asset, which can result in a prison term for the persons involved. By playing safe, the loan officers actually exaggerate the risks involved in lending to a small, private business or to one that is not clearly in a favored industry. In discussions[13] among economists the above argument is tied to the controversy over monetary policy in the late 1970s and early 1980s. Those who favored monetary restraint and higher interest rates to curb inflation believed that by fixing the interest rate at below the equilibrium level, the monetary authorities created an excess of demand over the supply of loanable funds. This disequilibrium leads to the segmentation of the loan market into a favored sector (for example, of large public enterprise borrowers) where all demand is satisfied and a nonpreferred sector where loans are rationed. Noneconomic criteria are introduced in the rationing process as a result— for example, special charges like "points," rebates, redeposits, and other favors. This entails the disuse of relative profitability as the criterion of allocating loanable funds among borrowers for different purposes, including savings among competing investments. One might go even further by arguing that the practice of using noneconomic criteria in allocating savings in the nonpreferred sector of borrowers may spill over to the preferred sector so that relative access to funds may become totally separated from relative efficiency and the future structure of the economy becomes distorted through the distortion of present choices of investments.

IMPROVING THE ALLOCATION AND USE OF SAVINGS

In view of the past performance of Taiwan's financial system and its existing institutions described above, the objective of improving the allocation of savings in accordance with the development plans consists of two principal tasks: (1) making the capital market more homogeneous and competitive, or less segmented, so that savings can earn the best returns available and are allocated to investments on the basis of relative productivity except where greater investments are to be channeled to specific directions, for example, high tech, in a measured manner but only as a result of deliberate policy and rational choice; (2) making such government intervention in the capital market least costly in terms of structural distortion.

On the first task the following ideas seem to follow logically:

First, greater competition among the banks can be stimulated by freer entry. The financial sector can be opened up to new private domestic banks. The government's legitimate concern about the growth of large financial-industrial-commercial interests akin to the Japanese *Zaibatsu* should be faced more directly and not be allowed to stymie the country's financial development. Competition can also be stimulated by expanding the permissible range of activities of foreign banks.

Second, the activities of banks in which there is partial government ownership can be made more innovative and supportive to business activity if ambiguity between a bad debt due to some unavoidable poor business judgment and a loss to a bank resulting from fraud or collusion on the part of its employees, and between the last cases and situations representing *potential* conflicts of interest. This may require another review of the revised Banking Law of 1975 as well as the criminal law governing fraud and the regulations pertaining to the employees of government-owned banks and other public enterprises and government agencies.

Third, in the interest of the individual and small business borrowers who have insufficient collaterals, a credit-rating and credit information system should be quickly developed. This applies equally to larger business borrowers and to the ranking of corporate bonds. The fact that Taiwan has begun to use credit cards of local origin suggests that such a credit-rating system may be about to appear and flourish.

Fourth, banks as a whole will become more competitive if better linkage between savers and the business users of capital can be established by making the securities market a more closely integrated part of all investment activities. Actually reform with this intent has been a topic of discussion in Taiwan for some time.

Finally, it goes without saying that a condition for reducing segmentation of the capital market, and thereafter avoiding its reemergence in a new guise, is to make sure that the price of borrowing money should be at its "natural" and equilibrium level of autonomous demand and supply. Overexpansion of aggregate spending—a central focus in Taiwan's 1982 public debate on monetary policy—

leads to an excess of credit demand. This can be followed either by a rise of the market interest rate[14] or by credit rationing in a submarket while demand in another more favored submarket is fully satisfied. Just as critics of Taiwan's financial market heretofore have suggested that small private business borrowers[15] fall into this category, "nonstrategic industries" in Taiwan's economic future could become the less favored sectors where credit rationing can emerge.

FINANCING OF HIGH TECH AND OTHER GROWTH INDUSTRIES

On the best manner of government intervention in financing selected knowledge-intensive and other growth industries that fit Taiwan's development policy, one theoretical issue deserves some discussion at this point. This concerns the manner in which such investment should be encouraged. Since we start from the premise that some of the beneficial effects of these investments, especially the indirect ones, are "external" and not included in the private financial returns the individual investors could anticipate to receive, government intervention is justified and aims at increasing the scale of such investments as well as the number of individual undertakings. In view of the previous discussion, it may be that such encouragement could better take the form of reduction of the business income tax rather than low-interest loans. Besides, any artificial reduction of the interest rate would alter relative factor-prices and might make the undertaking in question more capital-intensive than can be sustained in a volatile world market without continuing protection or other forms of public support. Accelerated depreciation in assessing taxable income might be another method of encouragement.

An income tax reduction scheme, however, would offer little inducement to a potential investor who does not anticipate any income. This raises the issue of assessing the probability of success of innovative, state-of-the-art enterprises. Assuming that private businessmen and savers overestimate a particular risk which the public authorities can assess more accurately, government participation through direct investment can be the only effective way to overcome the difficulty. However, how long the government should hold on to such investments before their resale to the public is another issue that needs to be resolved. The Development Fund of the Executive

Yuan mentioned earlier has up to now used both loans and direct stock participation in support of special projects. Our analysis would in theory lean to the side of government stock participation if the quality of management would be enhanced by it rather than adversely affected.

The assumption that the government can better estimate the success potential of R&D intensive and other strategic growth industries than private business needs to be examined further. It may be true that businessmen in many LDCs are unfamiliar with state-of-the-art products and processes and are content with running profitable operations and dealing with markets with which they are familiar. The same, however, can be said of many businessmen in developed countries. That this is the situation is obvious in view of the delayed structural adjustments facing certain U.S. and European manufacturing sectors and the painful problems the delay has caused them and their respective economies in the 1980s. It is also true that businesses in newly industrializing countries still hestitate to spend on R&D and to incur other long-term developmental costs that do not yield identifiable returns quickly. However, the fact that private business lags in this regard does not mean that the government will automatically succeed where the former fails. The conditions of success in anticipating the future and in minimizing the risk of failure must be examined more closely. Both the government and the public must be prepared for unavoidable failures and necessary adjustments.

REFORMING THE SECURITIES MARKET

The dominant role of banks as financial intermediaries in Taiwan is paralleled by the minor role played by the securities market. Stock and bond issues, relatively insignificant as they have been, have often been absorbed by the banks rather than the household sector. A major task facing the business community and policymakers alike is to develop the securities market as a means of mobilizing individual savings for continuing development. In the best case, new knowledge-intensive industries could bring significant gains to the investors and it would be beneficial to Taiwan's economic—and political—goals if such capital gains can be widely shared. In particular, access to such gains would help those who derive their income from the declining or more slowly growing sectors.

Of the 206,387 registered companies in Taiwan in 1983, the stocks of only 119 or 0.058 percent were listed on the Taipei stock exchange. The total capital of all the listed companies amounted to NT $166.2 billion or 11.54 percent of that of all the registered companies. Within the manufacturing sector only 81 of the 500 largest private firms were listed. During 1977-81, the total volume of new stocks issued, plus all public and corporate bond issues, including direct private placements with the banks, aggregated no more than 3.5 percent of the nation's GNP during the same period. This can be compared with an average ratio of gross domestic investment to GNP of 30 percent.[16]

The narrowness of the Taiwan stock market is a matter of long standing. The Taiwan Stock Exchange came into being in 1961; the Securities and Exchange Commission was first established in September 1960. Yet during the last decade, the number of listed companies grew only from 49 (1972) to 119 (November 1983). The existence of a strong resistance to public listing has been undeniable.

The number of share owners grew more rapidly during the same period, from 152,132 at the year end of 1972 to 594,118 at 1981 year end.[17] As of the end of 1982, 50.12 percent of the listed stocks were owned by individuals, 28.62 percent by government institutions, 21.26 percent by other organizations. No information is available on the length of time individual shareowners keep their stocks although in the opinion of some officials, there may be a preponderance of traders who are in the market for short-term gains. Of course, the small number of listed stocks tends to discourage some potential long-term investors.

The Securities and Exchange Commission was transferred to the jurisdiction of the Ministry of Finance from the Minister of Economic Affairs in July 1981. This seems to signify a policy of concentrating the task of revamping Taiwan's financial institutions under the Ministry of Finance. With its slightly expanded staff, the Commission has sharply stepped up its activity in making the securities market a more attractive and effective vehicle of direct investment for the savers and of long-term capital mobilization by business.

According to the SEC's 1983 annual report,[18] the Commission's present effort focuses on the protection of the private investor. Among the measures undertaken are increased close auditing of the listed companies' financial reports, with particular emphasis on inventory valuation and inspection, stricter regulation of the use of funds raised in new issues, insider trading, stock broker supervision, and so on. A program of public education of investors has been sponsored to explain investment in securities and to correct the popular image of "playing the market" and the common practice of following the large trader on the basis, unfortunately only too frequently, of rumors and tips. The collapse of three fairly widely known companies and the flight of some of their officers during the recent recession, not to mention the failure of a large credit union involving one of Taiwan's large financial groups, have added considerable impetus to the effort of the Finance Ministry to make the SEC a more vigilant watch dog and to rethink financial regulations. The work of investment consultants is also being encouraged.

It is in this connection that the role of the accountant and the integrity of the accounting profession as the guardian of truth in annual reports and financial statements has begun to arouse official attention as the importance of these reports becomes more keenly appreciated. The SEC has drafted new rules governing the auditing standards used by accountants and the certification of accounting firms engaged in public auditing. The Finance Ministry has also taken over the oversight of the accounting profession and has charged the Commission with the task of conducting a special study on accounting education, the certification and continuing education of accountants, accounting practice and standards, the role of the Society of Accountants and sanctions against errant members.

Another step in the promotion of investment in securities by the public has been the plan to develop investment trusts or mutual funds. This was first instituted through the establishment of an international investment company through which funds collected from outside Taiwan—in return for the trust company's own certificates of beneficial ownership—are used to purchase the stocks of listed companies on the Taipei Exchange. The regulations governing such funds are modeled after those of Japan, Korea, and OECD. The external aspect of such funds will be discussed more fully in Chapter 6. Domestic mutual funds will of course still be an intemediary form of investment for those savers who do not buy the stocks of individual firms directly. However, the investment company certificates will constitute a preliminary step before the inexperienced local saver plunges into individual stock ownership. The latter form of asset ownership may be more than a little risky when the investor is inexperienced and might expect a larger and faster return than is warranted by objective circumstances.

RISK-TAKING AND VENTURE CAPITAL INVESTMENT

Finally, the Ministry of Finance has proposed to use the investment company as a means of channeling savings to new investment in the high tech industries which Taiwan hopes to make into the core of its continuing economic progress. Shares in venture capital investment companies are the newest form of ownership being introduced in Taiwan. A venture capital investment company, under the recently enacted measure, will be given the greater corporate income tax exemption reserved for the most favored industrial and trading enterprises, exemption of personal income tax on dividends received by the stockholders of such companies, tax credit equal to a portion of their investments when the firms in question begin to earn profit, and so on. This form of investment is applicable not only to domestic investments by either domestic or foreign investors, but also by domestic investors placing investments abroad. As we shall see in Chapter 6, such investments in new R&D ventures abroad could become an effective way in technology acquisition.

The government-owned development banks and the Development Fund of the Executive Yuan are seen by Taiwan's financial authorities as the sources of seed money and of government participation in private ventures. Such a government role serves two purposes simultaneously: speeding up and increasing the scale of industrial development in selected sectors and increasing the number of listed stock issues on the local Exchange. The latter will help enhance the development of the securities market.

Common sense, as well as actual experience, however, tells us that some, perhaps many, new high tech firms will fail. There is always a shake-out period at the end of which the survivors of the initial trial and error and domestic as well as foreign competition will handsomely reward its steadfast or plain lucky owners. By investing in a number of such undertakings, but not too many at one time, a venture capital investment company can probably do quite well on the average. However, investors must be prepared for failures. Where government funds are involved, the practice that, according to some students, has hamstrung Taiwan's banking system and led to undue conservativeness must be averted. Hence we are once more faced with the need for attitudinal and behavioral change along with institutional adjustments and innovations.

Not the least important of course is the minimization of the risk of failure. If the participation of government capital lowers the risk for its private partners, the overall risk of failure is not reduced unless the government can claim better foresight and can command better management and more effective worldwide marketing, assuming Taiwan's dependence on the export market. Luck aside, what will have to be done to gain the greater and steadily improving knowledge base on which such management and marketing must be built? We turn next to the many facets of investment in human resources.

NOTES

1. See Chapter 7 on whether this issue of adequate savings might reappear.
2. One of the many other factors that will not be considered in this volume is income distribution except insofar as the latter might be affected by the distribution of returns from savings.
3. The data are taken from Paul C. H. Chiu, "Performance of Financial Institutions in Taiwan," *Proceedings of a Conference on Experiences and Lessons of Economic Development in Taiwan* (Taipei: The Institute of Economics, Academia Sinica, December 18-20, 1981), p. 434. The original data are derived from the Central Bank's 1980 study of the flow of funds in Taiwan.
4. Ibid., p. 433.
5. This aggregate excludes most short-term borrowing and borrowing from foreign banks and government institutions, the last being largely for purchasing imported equipment. It still includes some short-term investments from the "curb market".
6. The Central Bank averaged another 20.58 percent during this period, leaving the remaining 22.5 percent to the "medium and small business banks" (2.69 percent); credit cooperatives (5.35 percent); the credit departments of farmers' associations (3.51 percent); trust and investment companies (3.69 percent); the Postal Savings System (6.37 percent); and life insurance companies (0.94 percent). Since the deposits in postal savings were until 1983 remitted virtually entirely (93 percent according to Chiu, "Performance of Financial Institutions," p. 439) to the Central Bank for refinancing purposes, there is double counting in these figures. If the 6.37 percent of the postal savings system were eliminated, the adjusted average share of the domestic commercial banks would be 56.51 percent; that of all commercial banks would be 60.74 percent (ibid., p. 440).

7. The Bank of Communications was first established in Peking in 1907. Its head office was evacuated to Taipei in 1949. Operation was fully resumed in 1960.

8. Like the Bank of Communications, the Farmers Bank moved to Taiwan in 1949 and resumed full operation in May 1967.

9. The Central Trust undertakes multiple financial and related operations, including government procurement, insurance, transportation, warehousing, trading, etc. It was established in 1935 and came to Taiwan after World War II. The Postal Remittance and Savings Bank was established in 1930 and resumed operation in Taiwan in 1962.

10. These banks were reorganized from the former Taiwan Mutual Savings and Loan Company.

11. See, Li-teh Hsü, "Ching-yung ti shih-tai shi-ming" [The Mission of Finance in Our Time], *Tsai-shui Yen-chiu* [Studies in Finance] (Taipei), Vol. 15, No. 2, March 1, 1983, p. 6.

12. Ibid.

13. See Jia-dong Shea, "Taiwan chih Ching-yung T'i-hsi Shuang'yüan-hsin yü Kung-yeh Fa-chan" [The Dualistic Nature of Taiwan's Financial System and Industrial Development], *Conference Papers on Taiwan's Industrial Development, March 1983,* and *The Efficiency of Fund Allocations under Credit Rationing and Supply of Loans in the Dual Financial System in Taiwan* (Taipei: Chung-hua Institution for Economic Research, September 1983), Economic Papers No. 37.

14. This is what many U.S. economists and financial analysts mean when they argue that exceedingly large government borrowing to finance a huge federal deficit (projected in the 1984 and subsequent budgets) will lead to higher interest rates and the "crowding out" of private borrowers and therefore private investment spending.

15. We should add consumer credit users to this category in view of the lack of adequate credit rating facilities.

16. Given in a 1983 report by L. T. Hsü, the Minister of Finance, on the Taiwan stock market and its improvement. (Reprint from a press report, n.d.).

17. The Taiwan Stock Exchange, *Taiwan Stock Market: A Review of Its 20-year Performance* (Taiwan, n.d., probably 1983), p. 5. Minister Hsü's report gave the number of share owners in 1983 as 650,000.

18. *Tsai-cheng-pu Cheng-chüan-kuan-li-wei-yuan-hui Yeh-wu-pao-kao* [Business Report of the Securities and Exchange Commission, Ministry of Finance], December 14, 1983.

5

MEETING THE DEMAND FOR SCIENTIFIC AND TECHNICAL MANPOWER (S&T)

ECONOMIC DEVELOPMENT FROM THE PERSPECTIVE OF INTERINDUSTRY TRANSFERS OF LABOR

Economic development can be viewed as a continuing increase in per capita production over time accompanied by changes in the composition of the aggregate output. This structural change takes place as resources are shifted from less to more productive uses in response to changes in the demand and supply of productive factors and of the goods they produce. This is essentially the way in which some simplified, basic theoretical models explain economic development. For example, labor as a productive factor can be shifted from subsistence farming to a nonagricultural sector producing farm equipment. This process cannot get started without an injection of capital supplied either out of domestic savings (by curtailing actual or potential consumption) or through an inflow of foreign capital. Once this condition is satisfied, however, the development process will begin and it will continue as long as capital formation and the transfer of labor can proceed without interruption—until further structural change in this manner no longer pays as a result of diminishing returns and rising wages. At this point technological upgrading can be brought in to alter the absolute and relative productivities of the factors. When this happens, development will resume. This scenario does not envisage any difficulty attending to the movement of labor from the less to the more productive sectors.

The real world is far more complex. One complication stems from the imperfect substitutability of different factors of production in producing the same product or, to put the matter differently, from the unequal usefulness of the same factor in producing different products after moving from one sector to another. Nor are difficulties in mobility envisaged. This applies both to capital goods and labor. A designer of cars is not equivalent to a fraction of an automobile mechanic just as an oxygen furnace for smelting steel is not the equivalent of x locomotives. An illiterate peasant cannot become a farm machine maker overnight. Nor can a Ph.D. in aeronautics do research in genetic engineering. Furthermore, within each industry, specific kinds of labor and capital often have to be used in relatively fixed proportions. For instance, steel making and the manufacture of silicon wafers require quite different kinds of labor and capital equipment and there are in each case only a finite number of processes using specific kinds of labor, capital, and other inputs, in fixed or relatively fixed proportions. Hence a choice must first be made on the kinds of skilled manpower an economy should have in the future.

In the long run, this limited variability and substitutability can be changed, and the degree of change is determined by education, training, research, and development (R&D). The outcome of R&D depends in turn upon how a country uses its scientific and technological (S&T) capacity (including both manpower and plant) in both research and education. In the final analysis, therefore, the volume and nature of investment in S&T and educational manpower will determine the future supply of such manpower. Future additions to the existing stock of specialized manpower will determine whether supply will match the anticipated demand. The existing stock was determined by the educational and training system of the past while the present educational and training system will determine future supply. Export and import of talents will play a role in modifying domestic supply.

TAIWAN'S DEVELOPMENT NEEDS AND SUPPLY OF SPECIALIZED MANPOWER

The above theoretical framework can be used to analyze the supply and demand of specialized manpower for Taiwan's continuing development. Unless supply can match demand, development will be constrained. Conversely, if supply exceeds demand, unemployment and discontent may result. Besides, some of the investment in education and skilled manpower will have been wasted. In either case importation or exportation must be considered. Since recruitment from abroad and emigration of skilled professionals present far greater difficulties than does merchandise import or export, a substitute solution is to develop the import and export of professional services.

The problems of matching demand and supply can be further analyzed in a series of separate issues. In the first place, the quantity and kind of skilled manpower demanded can be examined from the point of view of the tasks it has to perform. Given an economy intent on making and selling new, higher value-added products in world markets, the critical tasks are R&D, production, marketing, and management. At the routine production level the demand is for engineers, technicians, and technically skilled workers. At the R&D level, S&T manpower is demanded for innovation at home and commercial adaptation of imported products and processes. A higher level of education and experience in general is needed for such personnel, including both scientists and engineers. Marketing talents and country and area specialists are needed if exporting to new geographical areas is to be expanded for the purpose of market diversification or for marketing new types of products in an otherwise established market. The same is true for the management of new industries or old industries selling new products and/or using new processes.[1] Given market diversification and production upgrading among Taiwan's principal development objectives, a large supply of talented forecasters adept at estimating demand in foreign markets and projecting future economic, legislative, and technical trends in S&T developments would be eminently useful.

In the second place, corresponding to each of the principal tasks mentioned above, the subject competence and level of education and training required will vary. Hence the supply of skilled manpower should be disaggregated according to specializations corresponding to demand. Figure 5.1, below presents an overview of this situation.

As far as government authorities are concerned, resolution of the above issues in Taiwan has fallen on the shoulders of quite a few agencies, including principally the Ministry of Education, the Bureau of Vocational Training in the Ministry of the Interior, the Council for Economic Planning and Development, the National Science Council (NSC), the Ministry of Economic Affairs, and the National Youth Commission. The bedrock of supply is the Ministry of Educa-

FIGURE 5.1. Demand for Skilled Manpower by Economic Function

Functions to Be Performed

		Upgrading of technical level of current production	R&D for new products and processes (including technology transfers)	Marketing of new products and in new geographical areas	New management organizations and methods; planning for noneconomic impact
Fields of training and special competence	For technical workers	Practical vocational training		Languages; area studies including detailed knowledge in special fields of production, foreign and domestic policies, laws, business practices, and so on	Management and social sciences; environmental studies
	For technical assistants	Ditto at a higher level			
	For R&D workers	Specialities by academic discipline and field in science and engineering			

tion which sets educational policy, oversees the activities of all the educational institutions, and through budget control determines the direction individual public and even private schools, colleges, and universities may follow. The Vocational Training Bureau, originally concerned mostly with employment training, has become increasingly occupied with technology transfer and the acquisition of special skills in the introduction and use of precision tools, equipment, and so on. A manpower group in the Council of Economic Planning and Development coordinates the manpower portion in the national economic forecast which resembles an indicative plan. It also heads a task force in the Cabinet that prods other agencies, including the Ministry of Education, in undertaking what the overall development program requires. The NSC and the Economic Affairs Ministry are concerned at the high end of R&D programs and technology transfers with helping the business and academic communities acquire specialists from abroad to meet the requirements of Taiwan institutions and to serve as trouble-shooters, for example, in popularizing automation and robotics. Finally, the National Youth Commission acts as a registry and employment exchange for returned Chinese graduate students from abroad in locating suitable employment in Taiwan.

ECONOMIC GROWTH AND ITS EDUCATIONAL INFRASTRUCTURE

Taiwan's economic growth record unquestionably owes a great deal to the quality of its labor force,[2] at the base of which are the schools, the infrastructure of education. Free elementary education was extended from six to nine years during the 1968-69 school year[3] when the economy was still in the early stage of its take-off. However, already in the 1964-65 school year, 96.83 percent of the population aged six to under 12 years (the elementary school age) were in school. (See Table 5.1.) This ratio rose to 99.79 percent in 1982-83. The number of students enrolled in junior high schools increased by 75 percent from 1967-68 to 1978-80 after the introduction of the nine-year free education system. The ratio of the population of the six to under-14 year cohort (primary and junior high school age) attending school rose more significantly, from 83.5 percent in 1964-65 and 85.5 percent in 1967-68 to 87.9 percent in 1968-69 and 99.7 percent in 1982-83.[4]

Beginning from the mid-1970s the absolute number of elementary school students began to show a steady decline, reflecting the slightly delayed effect of declining birth rates.[5] However, the junior high school population rose continuously, obviously encouraged by the extension of free education. Moreover, the data in Table 5.1 demonstrate a continuous improvement in the student to full-time teacher ratio. The latter declined at both the elementary and the junior high levels.

VOCATIONAL TRAINING AND HIGHER EDUCATION

Building upon the infrastructure, the growth of skilled manpower paralleled first the spurt of vocational education and then that at the university and college levels. Intermediate between the latter and the secondary level of senior high schools and senior vocational schools are the junior colleges (and polytechnics) which in Taiwan vary from

TABLE 5.1. Growth of Basic Education

	Number of Students (in thousands)		Number of Schools		Number of Full-time Teachers (in thousands)**		Percent of Population of Age 6-12 Years in School
	Elementary Schools	Junior High Schools	Elementary Schools	Junior High Schools	Elementary Schools	Junior High Schools	
1964/65	2,202.9	383.0	2,107	396*	51.9 (42.4)	18.2* (....)	96.83
1967/68	2,348.2	499.8	2,208	458*	55.7 (42.2)	23.7* (....)	97.52
1968/69	2,383.2	617.2	2,244	487	56.3 (42.3)	18.6 (33.2)	97.67
1969/70	2,428.0	710.8	2,275	525	57.9 (41.9)	22.7 (31.3)	97.62
1973/74	2,431.4	948.9	2,349	586	61.5 (39.5)	33.8 (28.1)	98.09
1978/79	2,278.7	1,082.1	2,412	632	68.4 (33.3)	42.3 (25.6)	99.64
1981/83	2,226.7	1,082.4	2,457	661	70.1 (31.8)	45.7 (23.7)	99.79

*Including senior high schools.
**The figures in parentheses are the numbers of students per full-time teacher.
Source: Ministry of Education, *Educational Statistics of the Republic of China* (Taipei, 1983), Tables 1, 2, 5, and 8; pp. 2–9, 18–21 and 28.

two to three years beyond the senior high school (and senior vocational school level) and are meant primarily to train technical workers and technicians. The sequence in which these events occurred and the growth patterns present an interesting correlation between the manpower development program and economic development in general.

In terms of students, the development of vocational education has followed changes on both the supply and the demand side. With increasing economic development and average income, Chinese parents who traditionally want their children to have a good education, if not a better one than their own, have begun to demand more schooling beyond the junior high and, later, also the senior high. On the other hand, the capacity of colleges and universities was limited and could not absorb more than a certain number of entrants each year. Nor would a primarily liberal arts college education be suitable to all young people or directly helpful in filling the developing job opportunities. The solution decided upon was an increase in vocational training and in junior college graduates. The economy's demand for technicians and for workers possessing increasing technical skills in the meantime grew and supplied more employment opportunities. The same was not equally true for all college and university graduates.

A very fast increase in the number of junior colleges and vocational schools occurred during the period of rapid economic growth (Table 5.2). The former grew by 245 percent in a five-year period, from 20 in 1964-65 to 69 in 1969-70, stabilizing subsequently at 76 in 1973-74.[6] The number of vocational schools rose by 40 percent between 1964-65 and 1973-74, increasing from 121 institutions in 1964-65 to 171 in 1973-74. Junior college enrollment also grew fastest during the 1964-65—1973-74 period, rising more than eight times, from 17,900 persons in 1964-65 to 147,600 persons in 1973-74. Vocational school enrollment grew by 117.8 percent but the increment in absolute numbers, 125,800 persons, was comparable to that of the junior colleges. Enrollment in the universities and in graduate schools at the master level also registered phenomenal rates of increase, 166.1 percent in university enrollment and 217 percent in master's programs; the absolute numbers were smaller. In 1973-74, undergraduate enrollment in Taiwan's universities numbered 120,300 persons; the corresponding number in 1964-65 was only 45,200. At the master's level, enrollment in 1973-74 was 2,745; in 1964-65 it was 866.

TABLE 5.2. Growth of Institutions of Vocational and Higher Education

School Year	Number of Institutions											Number of Students (in thousands)							
	Vocational Schools	Index	Junior Colleges	Index	Colleges	Index	Universities	Index	Colleges and Universities	Index	Vocational Schools	Index	Junior Colleges	Index	Universities	Index	M.A. Programs	Index	Ph.D. Programs	Index
1964/65	121	100.0	20	100.0	11	100.0	10	100.0	21	100.0	106.8	100.0	17.9	100.0	45.2	100.0	866	100.0	18	100.0
1969/70	141	116.5	69	345.0	13	118.2	9	90.0	22	104.8	155.9	146.0	96.0	536.3	86.2	190.7	1,856	214.3	138	766.7
1973/74	171	141.3	76	380.0	14	127.3	9	90.0	23	109.5	232.6	217.8	147.6	824.6	120.3	266.1	2,745	317.0	225	1,250.0
1978/79	184	152.1	75	375.0	17	154.5	9	90.0	26	123.8	312.1	292.2	166.5	930.2	145.2	321.2	4,974	574.4	469	2,605.5
1982/83	202	166.9	77	395.0	12	109.1	16	160.0	28	133.3	394.3	369.2	203.7	1,138.0	163.5	361.7	7,517	867.8	975	5,416.7

*Including senior high schools.
Source: Ministry of Education, Educational Statistics of the Republic of China (Taipei, 1983), Tables 1, 2, 5, and 8; pp. 2–9, 18–21 and 28.

The years after 1973-74 represented a new phase of educational development in Taiwan. Two distinguishing features are discernible. First, in terms of institutional expansion, the total number of universities and colleges—the latter having fewer departments and specialized schools—grew by five or from 23 to 28, partly through the upgrading of some colleges after internal expansion. Second, there was a very large increase in enrollment at the graduate level, from 2,745 (1973-74) to 7,517 (1982-83) persons or an increase of 173.8 percent in M.A. programs and from 225 (1973-74) to 975 (1982-83) or 333.3 percent in Ph.D. programs. Otherwise, the upward trend in enrollment continued in vocational schools while that in both junior colleges and universities had visibly slowed down.

EDUCATIONAL EXPENDITURE AND DEVELOPMENT POLICY

Although a significant private sector exists in both middle level and higher education in Taiwan, tax-supported schools and universities dominate in size and number of departments. Public expenditure on education, therefore, is a good indicator of the government's long-term policy in economic development on the assumption that reality will eventually make any large discrepancy between demand and supply in specific categories of manpower intolerable to decision makers eager to promote development. The relative shares in total spending on education enjoyed by the different categories of institutions and their aggregate spending as a ratio of the government budget and the GNP respectively will further illustrate the government's apparent effort to coordinate education with development policy and some of the problems it must have faced.

Table 5.3 illustrates very clearly the large relative share in total spending on education accounted for by the nine-year free schooling children in Taiwan receive. Until total expenditure on education was raised very substantially in 1981-82 (bearing in mind, however, the price inflation in 1973-74 and 1979-81), this share stood at 40 percent or above of the total. The share of colleges and universities in the total educational budget, therefore, did not rise until the 1979-80 academic year. Budgeted spending in this category actually fell relatively from 1976-77 to 1978-79 in spite of an increasing budget in current NT dollars. The graduate school programs that grew

TABLE 5.3. Public and Private Educational Expenditures in Relation to Total Government Spending and the GNP

Public and Private Educational Expenditure by Category	Total NT$ million		Percent					Public Educational Spending as Percent of Total Government Expenditure	Budgeted Spending of Public Educational Institutions as a Multiple of That of Private Institutions	Ratio of Total Expenditure on Education to GNP
			Nine-year Free Education	Senior Vocational Schools	Junior Colleges	Colleges and Universities	Other*			
1964/65	3,152.3	100.0	—	—		18.3**		13.3	4.5	3.4
1968/69	7,347.5	100.0	—	—		22.5**		16.4	4.9	4.0
1969/70	8,697.7	100.0	—	—		24.5**		16.5	5.1	4.1
1973/74	14,743.2	100.0	48.0	9.0		21.9**		13.9	3.5	3.2
1978/79	43,269.6	100.0	48.8	9.2	7.5	11.8		14.3	4.5	4.1
1981/82	94,673.7	100.0	39.5	9.1	8.4	14.0		15.1	4.6	5.4

*Included under "other" are pre-school, senior high school and social education expenditures, educational administration, international cultural exchange and other items not listed in the original source.
**Combined percent for junior colleges and senior colleges and universities.
Source: Ministry of Education, *Educational Statistics of the Republic of China* (Taipei, 1983), Tables 1, 2, 5, and 8; pp. 38–41.

through the 1970s both institutionally and in student enrollment, therefore, might have done so more vigorously if they had been better financed. Finally, the more rapid increase in spending by the public educational institutions in comparison with that of the private educational sector suggests also that perhaps much more could have been done by the business community at the university level and in sponsoring graduate studies and research. To date, businessmen have apparently been much more active at the junior college level than in higher education and R&D, and that may be the combined result of what the higher educational institutions have been able to offer and what the business community perceives to be its need.

INSTITUTIONAL COORDINATION AND ADJUSTMENT IN MANPOWER PLANNING

The preceding account of the developments of the educational system at various levels does not enable us to draw an unambiguous conclusion on the efficacy of coordination between education planning and manpower development since 1965. On the one hand, the sequence in which vocational schools, junior colleges, and universities have succeeded one another in expansion impresses the observer as well coordinated with the requirements of development planning. On the other hand, the need to upgrade the technological level of production in general, to transfer technology from abroad, and to stimulate domestic R&D and innovation on a commercial scale, appears to have been reflected in the educational system always more than a little belatedly. Anticipation of the changing demand, admittedly, has been difficult. Whether this has in fact been the case and why can be explored by reviewing some of the comments of the Council on Economic Development and Planning in its appraisal of the manpower planning program.[7]

According to the Council's studies,[8] technical manpower at the junior college level was, as of 1983, in surplus. At the university level, while surpluses existed in the physical and agricultural sciences, there was a manpower shortage in medicine and engineering. At the graduate level there was a general shortage, but especially in certain categories of engineering. This shortage was attributed to limitations of equipment, personnel, academic rules, and rigidities in the existing educational system. The last constraints had led to low efficiency in the utilization of both plant and faculty. A large increase in the number of engineering departments at the university level had proved insufficient to meet the demand for graduates from engineering. Yet at the same time admission rules had not actually resulted in an increase in new entrants to those departments where the demand for graduates was high. Other adverse comments included poor standards in some junior colleges, inadequate practical as against theoretical knowledge in some of the physical sciences, insufficient communication and exchange between the industrial/business community and the academies, and so on.

These criticisms sound familiar to observers who have witnessed the mutual suspicion in other countries, especially LDCs, between those whose emphasis is on economic and technical practicality and those who think of the aim of education as primarily cultivation of the intellect. Some of the apparent slowness of the educational establishment to respond to the demands of current economic development goals is probably pure bureaucratic rigidity. Yet there is at least an element of the traditional conflict one finds between liberal arts and professional schools.

However, one inherent issue goes deeper. In estimating the demand for specialists in various fields, the general approach followed by forecasters is to start with some postulated GDP growth rate. The postulated GDP of a future date is then broken down into output and input sectors via an input-output table, and finally into labor inputs of different disciplines at technical levels. The trouble is that the input coefficients and output categories are by necessity based on historical experience. Where the external economic conditions, such as energy prices, have changed rapidly, past input-output relations become an extremely misleading guide.

In the case of Taiwan, extreme dependence on external markets that should be diversified and a general desire for new technologies make businessmen extremely sensitive to conditions in other markets, and forecasting of foreign political and economic conditions is no less important than that of new technological trends. Yet, curiously, such forecasting has not been emphasized. Nor have foreign language and practical and detailed area studies been stressed, Spanish being perhaps an exception. Some critics believe that the quality of junior college graduates is too low; some complain about over-expansion, which would of course have a tendency to lower quality. By the same token, poor foreign language training may be the cause of difficulty in finding employment. There is no real surplus of qualified foreign language and country specialists. It seems that too little emphasis has been placed on the demand side of expanding exports and on supplying skilled personnel in foreign areas and external marketing aside from future technologies.

According to the Council's estimates in 1982 and 1983, shortages will persist at the graduate level, for example, in mechanical, electrical, and electronic engineering. A long time lag, however, separates future demand from the students of today who will be coming out of graduate work to satisfy the postulated demand. There really is no way to eliminate the inherent uncertainty in matching demand and supply.

Perhaps a solution lies (1) in increasing the flexibility and substitutability of skilled technicians and scientists, (2) in increasing the role of both export and import of such personnel, and (3) in greater involvement of the private sector in business-sponsored and in-industry training. The last course of action may actually lead to greater private R&D funding. A number of measures such as in-service training and educational programs, the institution of night and summer schools and special institutes to utilize the existing faculty and plant more fairly, sabbaticals for broadening experience and knowledge (in industry for the teachers and in academic institutions for the technical employees of business) and the annual re-evaluation of course contents and requirements for various specializations all point in the same direction as (1). They are among the recommendations of the manpower group of the Council for Economic Planning and Development.

The second and third measures are really correlated. Industrial and other business concerns may be closer to the trends of future technologies. The same can perhaps be said of experienced scientists and technicians at the state-of-the-art level. The former, however, may be short-sighted and unwilling to invest heavily in manpower development out of fear that competitors might reap the benefit. They may prefer, therefore, to raid others in order to satisfy their own need. In this case, the traditional approach is to import foreign talent or to recruit Chinese talent from abroad when a serious supply shortage emerges. An alternative approach is to make sure that future shortages will not appear by expanding supply in certain categories at a possible cost of excess supply. Over-supply will have to be relieved then by encouraging export or emigration when a surplus really arises. However, the public purse will then have to make much larger investments in developing highly trained and costly S&T specialists.

FOREIGN BUSINESS PARTICIPATION IN TRAINING TECHNICAL WORKERS

Among the most innovative measures adopted in upgrading technical manpower has been the contracting of two European firms for training technical workers. The initial program, conceptually borrowed from Singapore and dated back to mid-year 1980, was the first major project of the Vocational Training Agency established in March 1981. Precision machine workers were selected after a questionnaire survey as the focus of the first project with Philips of Holland. A second project with Siemens of West Germany focuses on electric and electronic workers. Both aim at providing three-year training for high school graduates after the completion of their military service and include one year's in-training at cooperating firms.[9]

While this program is far too new for us to assess its results, a priori, its benefits to both Taiwan and the participating Dutch and German firms are obvious. The trainees who also take courses on the side and receive vocational school diplomas will obtain professional certification and thereby help set up a system of professional standards. This is in line with the general policy of developing standards and quality control.

Participation of technical workers in domestic and international demonstrations and contests of skills will also help develop the public's general respect for good workmanship and the country's reputation for it abroad. The foreign firms like Philips and Siemens presumably will not suffer from the fact that the trainees, who will no doubt be counted among the elite technical workers of the country, will be most familiar with their respective products. That future export sales are a major factor in the foreign firms' concerns has additional ramifications that will be discussed in the next chapter.

UNRESOLVED ISSUES

The preceding discussion has shown a wide ranging series of adjustments and new undertakings in skilled manpower development at all levels. The ROC authorities responsible for planning these activities appear to have come to grips with virtually all the issues. An outside observer can only point to certain issues that seem to defy clear-cut solutions. The existence in a continuously changing world of diverse categories of knowledge and skills most of which can be acquired only after a lengthy gestation period in the form of education and training make the task of matching demand and supply unavoidably difficult. One should not perhaps hope to reach a path of dynamic equilibrium. Rather, it seems, one should try to devise means of increasing the economy's ability to adjust. Human capital, like material capital goods, must not be allowed to become inflexible vested and economic interests blocking future adjustments of the economic structure. Aside from increasing the possibility of acquiring new capabilities through "retraining" facilities—in the broad sense—for a small trade-oriented economy like Taiwan, the obvious solution is foreign trade, that is, foreign trade in services of knowledge. Chapter 3 has already discussed certain aspects of this issue on the import side in the sense of recruiting talents from outside Taiwan. The export side will be addressed in Chapter 6.

NOTES

1. Even in the United States, management in some old line electric utilities, for instance, has proved to be incompetent in building and running nuclear power plants.

2. The data cited here are taken from the 1983 edition of *Educational Statistics of the Republic of China* (Taipei: Ministry of Education, 1983), pp. 2-27.

3. The academic or school year begins on August 1 and ends on July 31 of the following year. For instance, the 1983-84 academic year begins on August 1, 1983 and ends on July 31, 1984, and is known as the 1983 academic year.

4. Directorate-General of Budget, Accounting and Statistics, Executive Yuan, *Statistical Yearbook of the Republic of China* (Taipei: 1983), p. 363.

5. Ibid., p. 3.

6. While the Ministry of Education's *Statistical Yearbook* (Note 4) contains a great deal of factual data, the reader should refer to Research Group on Educational System Reform, *Hsüeh-chih Kai-ke* [Educational System Reform] (Taipei: Ministry of Education, 1983 Draft Plan), which contains an account of the conceptual background underlying the attempts to relate education to skilled manpower supply and economic development.

7. See *Taiwan Ching-chi-chien-she Shih-nien-chi-hua: Jen-li Fa-chan Pu-men Chi-hua, 1980-1989* [Taiwan's Ten-year Economic Development Plan, 1980–

1989 Manpower Plan] (Taipei: Council for Economic Planning and Development, September, 1980).

8. Courtesy of CEPD briefings in 1983-84.

9. See *Nei-cheng-pu Chih-yeh-hsün-lien-chü Nien-pao* [Annual Report of the Bureau of Vocational Training] (Taipei: 1983).

6

LIBERALIZATION OF THE EXTERNAL ECONOMY AND INTERNATIONALIZATION

BROADENING OF EXTERNAL ECONOMIC RELATIONS

From the external economic perspective, a principal concern of continuing growth is the expansion of foreign markets in order to absorb the country's increasing capacity to produce goods and services. Both labor and capital need employment and both are continually augmented, qualitatively no less than quantitatively, by investment—which must be forthcoming to absorb increasing savings—and by increase in productivity on which continuing competitiveness in the world must be based. Complementary to market expansion is the need for an increasing and secure supply of imported resources without which neither exports nor production for the domestic market can hope to increase with efficiency and comparative advantage in relation to the rest of the world. Therefore, continuation of economic growth is inevitably tied to the broadening of the country's relations with the rest of the world. This is true especially for an island economy. The word "broadening" is used to signify the multiplication of the economy's relations with other nations, both by kind of transactions and by number of partners, and the changing role the country plays in the international economy as a result.

Although foreign trade expansion is of paramount importance, it is by no means the sole external economic issue. For an economy like Taiwan which has seen its total external merchandise trade rise very sharply, from $968.4 million in 1965, when U.S. economic aid ended, to $8,275 million in 1973, when the first oil crisis broke, and again to $45,410 million in 1983, other external transactions too have inevitably begun to assume major importance. Questions about such current account items as the payment and receipt of interest and dividends and unilateral transfers can no longer be ignored. Do their magnitudes make economic sense? Are they of "normal" proportions? Do they contain economic and perhaps political significance that should be addressed by policy makers?

At the stage of economic development Taiwan has reached, investments in foreign countries by its businessmen and ordinary citizens have begun to develop of their own accord. Some businesses may wish to expand foreign sales by producing abroad closer to raw material supply and/or behind foreign tariff and other protective walls. Others may wish to secure import supplies for domestic production and export and carve out a share of a larger regional or global market. To some business investors purchasing a foreign interest may be the best way of acquiring foreign technology. For individual investors, foreign investment may simply be good financial management through portfolio diversification. If there is a concomitant emigration of persons, outward flows of capital in the form of unilateral transfers should be expected as a matter of course.[1]

The expanding external economic relations of a growing economy does not stop with increases in the usual balance of payments items. The role it plays in its relations with other nations also changes. Two of the Western Pacific's NICs—Singapore and Hong Kong—have risen to their economic preeminence first as entrepôts and then as regional trade, financial, and manufacturing centers. Taiwan does not have the same geographical advantage as these two city economies but it possesses other advantages, such as a large and growing supply of technical labor force and a sizeable domestic market of 18 million people whose incomes and expenditures are rising rapidly. These are, however, only the more obvious advantages. The potential change in Hong King's economic status in or around 1997 poses the threat of its impending inability to perform its usual international financial, merchandizing and manufacturing roles, thus creating a regional vacuum that others will try to fill. This opens up new regional and global economic functions Taiwan might just be able to provide.

The broadening of external economic relations between Taiwan and the rest of the world stems in part from the rupture of diplomatic ties with the United States. The Taiwan authorities have had to substitute economic and business relations for conventional diplo-

EXPORT EXPANSION AND STRUCTURAL CHANGE

A glance at the magnitude and composition of Taiwan's external commerce, especially since 1979, would help in understanding some of the trade issues the country faces. The period after 1979 is particularly important because it includes the years of worldwide recession and recovery at the beginning of the 1980s and because 1979 was for the Republic of China a traumatic year in its diplomatic history.

Formal diplomatic relations with the United States were severed in that year and it looked then as if the country which was Taiwan's ally for nearly 40 years had cut the island republic adrift. Yet Table 6.1 shows that Taiwan's exports in current dollars rose continuously from 1979 onward in spite of the second major oil price hike by OPEC, the political shock of U.S. derecognition, and recession in foreign markets. The lowest annual growth rate of 4.2 percent in terms of NT Dollars was registered in 1982. (In U.S. dollars there was a de-

TABLE 6.1. Growth of Merchandise Exports and Imports, 1965, 1973, and 1979-83 (in million US $)

	Exports		Imports	
	Value	Index (1965 = 100)	Value	Index (1965 = 100)
1965	450	100.0	556	100.00
1973	4,483	996.2	3,792	682.0
1979	16,103	3,578.4	14,774	2,657.2
1980	19,811	4,402.4	19,733	3,549.1
1981	22,611	5,024.6	21,200	3,812.9
1982*	22,204	4,934.2	18,888	3,397.1
1983	25,123	5,582.9*	20,287	3,608.7

*Preliminary.
Source: Council for Economic Planning & Development, Executive Yuan, *Taiwan Statistical Data Book 1983* (Taiwan: 1983), pp. 186-187.

cline of 1.8 percent in that year.) But only a year later, Taiwan's exports were able to regain their stride, rising at 13.1 percent per annum. (The years of 1965, when U.S. economic aid to Taiwan ended, and of 1973, the year of OPEC's oil embargo, have been included in the table in order to remind the reader of how far the Taiwan economy has come since those days.)

Table 6.2 shows changes in the commodity composition of exports. While the record of 1965-73 presented a graphic illustration of

TABLE 6.2. Composition of Exports (in percent)

	Total	Agricultural Products	Processed Agricultural Products	Industrial Products
1965	100.0	23.6	30.4	46.0
1973	100.0	7.5	7.9	84.6
1979	100.0	4.4	5.1	90.5
1980	100.0	3.6	5.6	90.8
1981	100.0	2.4	5.4	92.2
1982	100.0	1.9	5.7	92.4

Source: *Taiwan Statistical Data Book 1983*, p. 189.

Taiwan's transition from an LDC to an NIC, as shown by the relative increase in industrial exports and the sharp decline of agricultural exports,[2] for our purpose attention should be focused on the continued structural change since 1979. The economic objective of structural change, emphasized time and again by government officials and academicians, has been in part a response to the exigencies of international politics at the turn of the decade. Within the group of industrial exports, textiles, at $5,226 million, topped the list in 1979. It was followed by "electrical machinery and apparatus," at $2,775 million. In 1983, just four years later, electrical machinery and apparatus had risen to the top place at $4,851 million, including $3,775 million of electronic products. Textiles, on the other hand, had fallen to $4,599 million. Nonelectric machine exports, which in 1979 amounted to $608 million, had come up to $966 million. These changes prompted the Council for Economic Planning and Development to remark in January 1984[3] that the desired structural readjustment did in fact manage to continue through the recession years and should be attributed to a sharp increase in labor productivity that exceeded by a large margin the rise of wages.

Export sales by manufacturers in the Hsinchu Science-based Industry Park grew from $3.5 million in 1981 to $25.7 million in 1982 and $83.2 million in the first 11 months of 1983.[4] While this growth record appeared impressive for a still new project, the structural change in total exports toward more knowledge-intensive products up to 1983 was evidently not the direct accomplishment of H.S.I.P. alone but one of the broader drive to promote electronics and the information industry as a "strategic industry."

TABLE 6.3. Distribution of Taiwan's Exports (f.o.b.) by Country (in percent)

	1965	1973	1979	1982
United States	21.33	37.41	35.10	39.46
Hong Kong	6.21	6.60	7.08	7.04
Japan	30.60	18.37	13.96	10.71
Western Europe				
Belgium	0.52	0.66	0.71	0.60
Netherlands	1.34	1.99	2.11	1.47
France	0.19	0.53	1.18	1.12
Italy	0.54	1.16	1.21	0.92
West Germany	6.57	4.80	4.61	3.55
United Kingdom	0.77	2.51	2.52	2.38
Subtotal	9.93	11.65	12.34	10.04
ASEAN				
Indonesia	–	2.64	2.48	1.91
Malaysia	1.23	0.69	0.81	1.00
Philippines	1.38	0.65	1.25	1.06
Singapore	2.05	2.89	2.62	2.60
Thailand	3.67	1.42	1.15	0.97
Subtotal	8.33	8.29	8.31	7.54
Other	24.20	17.68	23.21	25.21
Total	100.00	100.00	100.00	100.00

Source: Directorate-General of Budget, Accounting and Statistics, Executive Yuan, *Statistical Yearbook of the Republic of China 1983* (Taiwan: 1983), pp. 180–181.

The development of more and more technology-intensive exports as they come closer to state-of-the-art levels is clearly time-consuming. Consequently, other channels of export expansion deserve attention, especially if they seem to have been under-emphasized. A most obvious point is revealed in Table 6.3 which shows the relative neglect of the European market by Taiwan.

DIVERSIFICATION OF EXPORT MARKETS

What about diversification of export markets? During 1965-73, the relative importance of the United States rose from 21.3 percent of Taiwan's total merchandise exports to 37.4 percent, an increase of over 70 percent. The relative share of the principal Common Market countries, at about 9 percent in total remained stationary as did the ASEAN members and Hong Kong, which are among Taiwan's nearest neighbors. The growth of the U.S. market during the Vietnam War and American economic expansion was entirely understandable; the decline of Japan's share was perhaps equally so. The failure of a greater relative expansion of sales to the other regional markets was certainly disappointing.

During 1973-79, Taiwan's initial effort to diversify export markets appeared to be showing some partial results as the shares of Western Europe increased slightly along with a relative expansion of sales to other markets not detailed in Table 6.3, such as Saudi Arabia, several Latin American countries, and South Africa. But the overall picture was marred by the failure of the expansion of sales on the Japanese market pari passu with the rise of Taiwan's overall exports which, like world trade as a whole, were inflated in value by large price increases in the 1970s.

From 1979 to 1982, thanks to the worldwide recession and the swifter U.S. emergence out of it than most other developed economies, and to the balance of payments difficulties and external indebtedness of many developing countries that reduced their imports, Taiwan's export diversification efforts were dealt a counterblow. In relative terms, contrary to the hopes of economic policy makers, the United States market became even more important than before; the individual shares of Western Europe, ASEAN, and Japan all declined. "Other" destinations, including Saudi Arabia, Kuwait, and South Africa, offered some slight compensation. The general trend, however, moved toward greater concentration rather than less.

One should not lose sight of the fact that the reversal in market diversification hopes in 1979-82 took place under adverse economic conditions in precisely those countries where Taiwan tried to increase exports relatively and that total exports in all markets were nevertheless still growing. Hence, in the short run, failure to develop exports more vigorously in some markets, such as Japan[5] and Western Europe,[6] was more than offset by unusually strong expansion in other markets, notably the United States. However, in the long run, market diversification as a policy must certainly be pursued much more vigorously than heretofore.

The problems confronting Taiwan's exports in different markets are not the same. In the United States, some of Taiwan's exports are more than competitive. They, however, face increasing protectionist challenges. Textiles are a good example. Other exports to the United States face strong competition from suppliers of lower labor cost, for example, some men's underwear which South Korea and Hong Kong are able to supply at progressively lower prices. During its colonial days in Taiwan, Japan cultivated the island as a source of agricultural goods and subtropical products—for example, rice, sugar, pineapples, and bananas. In recent decades Japan has tried to use Taiwan as a source of production and assembly based on cheaper labor supply while continuing to import "agricultural- (including marine-) based" products. To increase exports to Japan, Taiwan must therefore diversify into nontraditional exports.

In all cases, however, Taiwan's common shortcoming appears to be insufficient marketing and product identification.[7] An effort to develop trading companies of the Japanese model has not been successful so far. Many European countries also know relatively little about Taiwan. Furthermore, some may be too intimidated by the PRC to expand trade and other relations with Taiwan,[8] fearing that they might then lose a lucrative potential China market. One syllogism seems to run as follows: We could and probably would buy more from Taiwan if we could sell more in return. (This is the usual bilateral balance argument.) But selling more goods to Taiwan that Taiwan really wants (for example, arms) would incur the wrath of a 1 billion-customer market. Ergo, keep the market shut to Taiwan products. However, resistance based on ignorance can probably be overcome by more vigorous marketing and by increased purchases in Europe on Taiwan's part, which is already happening.

Table 6.4 shows the share Taiwan accounted for in recent years

TABLE 6.4. Total Imports of Selected Developed Economies and Taiwan's Share
(value in million dollars, Taiwan's share in percent)

	1965 Taiwan	1965 World	1965 Taiwan's Share	1973 Taiwan	1973 World	1973 Taiwan's Share	1979 Taiwan	1979 World	1979 Taiwan's Share	1981 Taiwan	1981 World	1981 Taiwan's Share
United States	93.2	21,366.4	0.44	1,783.6	69,477.1	2.57	6,426.6	217,462.2	2.95	8,631.2	271,212.7	3.18
Japan	157.3	8,169.0	1.92	883.7	38,134.4	2.32	2,475.6	110,108.4	2.25	2,522.5	140,830.3	1.79
Western Europe												
Belgium-Luxembourg	1.3	6,373.6	0.02	26.3	21,820.1	0.12	92.2	60,185.8	0.15	117.5	61,448.4	0.19
Netherlands	2.2	7,462.2	0.03	68.4	23,534.2	0.29	269.1	66,926.7	0.40	323.8	65,664.4	0.49
France	2.5	10,335.9	0.02	37.1	36,773.1	0.10	294.0	106,711.0	0.27	402.6	120,278.6	0.33
Italy	2.1	7,347.3	0.03	58.7	27,845.5	0.21	239.9	76,474.0	0.31	279.7	88,999.0	0.31
West Germany	30.0	17,472.2	0.17	229.1	54,495.6	0.42	879.1	157,681.9	0.56	1,063.2	162,691.2	0.65
United Kingdom	3.7	16,137.7	0.02	127.5	38,875.1	0.33	462.2	102,505.9	0.45	647.0	101,687.5	0.64

Source: OECD, *Foreign Trade by Commodities*, Series C, Paris, various issues.

as a supplier of imports to seven European countries. While its share in each case increased between 1973 and 1979, and, with the exception of Italy, again between 1979 and 1981, the relative proportion Taiwan enjoyed in 1981 was, in the maximal case of West Germany, no more than 0.65 of 1 percent of total German imports. This compares with 3.18 percent of the United States and a minuscule 1.79 percent for Japan, considering the geographical proximity between Japan and Taiwan. While protectionist sentiments may play a role in imports of special items, in general, one can safely assume that Taiwan's failure to make a larger inroad in Western European markets, thus making the European nations relatively unimportant trading partners of Taiwan, is a result of, either the uncompetitiveness of Taiwan products, or European unfamiliarity with them, or both. This raises again the issue of marketing and the need for greater savoir-faire about the European business community. Lag in European studies in the educational system, as noted in the preceding chapter, goes hand in hand with poor commercial intelligence, untimeliness of response to opportunities which probably go unrecognized in the first place and inadequate marketing. On its part Western Europe's failure to keep up its commercial ties with Taiwan after its diplomatic recognition of Peking has hurt itself as well as Taiwan. However, during 1980-81, a number of British, French, and Dutch banks set up either branches or representatives' offices in Taipei so that credit information at least ceased to be a monopoly of U.S. banks. European and ROC economic and cultural offices have also been set up in Taipei and Europe respectively after the Europeans finally learned from the U.S. example that trade with Taiwan could indeed prosper without formal diplomatic relations, and that the PRC market was still barely on the horizon.

The task of market diversification for exports is closely tied to existing bilateral trade balances. While there is no economic justification at all why multilateral trade should result in exact bilateral balance between any pair of nations, the side experiencing a persistent trade deficit almost always uses it as an argument in trade negotiation to demand import liberalization from the other side. The country distribution of Taiwan's imports (see Table 6.5) shows quite clearly the declining shares of both the United States and Japan as suppliers of Taiwan's imports over the years. Since the figures are greatly distorted by the spectacular oil price increase and, therefore, the larger shares taken by the oil exporters—shown under "other" in Table 6.5, the really significant change over time has been the increased share of the United States relative to that of Japan. While the shares of both declined after 1973 vis-à-vis "other" countries, the United States did a great deal better than Japan. Nevertheless, over the years, Taiwan's

TABLE 6.5. Distribution of Taiwan's Imports (c.i.f.) by Country (in percent)

	1965	1973	1979	1982
United States	31.72	25.27	22.90	24.13
Hong Kong	1.04	2.64	1.39	1.63
Japan	39.80	37.92	30.90	25.30
Western Europe				
Belgium	0.19	0.61	0.59	0.30
Netherlands	0.72	1.11	0.75	0.84
France	0.39	0.74	0.82	1.67
Italy	1.06	0.74	1.00	0.99
West Germany	3.07	5.39	4.31	4.16
United Kingdom	1.55	1.94	2.01	1.43
Subtotal	6.98	10.53	9.48	10.39
ASEAN				
Indonesia	0.03	2.69	3.06	1.37
Malaysia	1.14	1.65	2.23	2.49
Philippines	2.38	1.47	0.50	0.36
Singapore	0.48	0.71	0.84	0.80
Thailand	0.94	1.51	0.46	0.56
Subtotal	4.97	8.03	7.09	5.58
Other	15.49	15.61	28.24	32.97
Total	100.00	100.00	100.00	100.00

Source: Directorate-General of Budget, Accounting and Statistics, Executive Yuan, *Statistical Yearbook of the Republic of China 1983* (Taiwan: 1983), pp. 180–181.

trade surplus with the United States has increased along with its deficit with Japan. Taiwan is, however, still a more important market to Japan than it is to the United States, which is, however, catching up rapidly (see Table 6.6).

TABLE 6.6. Total Exports of Selected Developed Countries and Taiwan's Share (value in million dollars, Taiwan's share in percent)

	1965			1973			1979			1981		
	Taiwan	World	Taiwan's Share	Taiwan	World	Taiwan's Share	Taiwan	World	Taiwan's Share	Taiwan	World	Taiwan's Share
United States	438.6	27,003.3	1.62	1,095.1	70,246.0	1.56	3,149.9	173,648.9	1.81	4,135.5	225,776.5	1.83
Japan	217.9	8,451.8	2.56	1,635.0	36,771.8	4.45	4,365.0	102,964.4	4.24	5,400.3	151,910.1	3.55
Western Europe												
Belgium-Luxembourg	1.2	6,381.7	0.02	24.9	22,272.0	0.11	70.2	56,083.2	0.12	46.8	55,237.9	0.08
Netherlands	3.7	6,393.3	0.06	42.2	23,844.0	0.18	96.6	63,389.2	0.15	89.6	68,313.2	0.13
Italy	4.1	7,188.0	0.06	34.7	22,261.4	0.15	115.9	73,249.5	0.16	141.9	75,302.7	0.19
France	2.1	10,048.2	0.02	31.9	35,378.5	0.09	90.6	97,958.8	0.09	139.3	101,246.2	0.14
West Germany	15.9	17,892.3	0.09	226.2	67,436.9	0.33	504.6	171,436.7	0.29	531.3	175,284.3	0.30
United Kingdom	4.8	13,226.7	0.04	59.8	30,540.0	0.19	215.8	90,508.3	0.24	232.0	98,860.7	0.23

Source: OECD, *Foreign Trade by Commodities*, Series C, Paris, various issues.

LIBERALIZATION AND CHANGES IN THE TRADING SYSTEM

As Taiwan's external trade expands with economic growth, the environment of trade also changes. The volume and nature of trade in turn change with the environment and become a part of the changing world trade system. Thus, the increasing share Taiwan accounts for in U.S. imports has further stimulated American interest in Taiwan as a major source of low-priced manufactures. At the same time, in view of the mounting merchandise trade deficit of the United States in the early 1980s, including a significant one in favor of Taiwan, the general U.S. policy of export promotion has also included Taiwan among the targeted markets in Asia, with Japan of course heading the list. A generally liberal free-trade policy, advocated by the Office of the Special Trade Representative has thus been accompanied by industry demands for import quotas, charges of unfair competition and dumping, and, from time to time, the imposition of countervailing duties. As one of the leading countries which have benefited from the Generalized Special Preference system of zero tariffs for selected commodities within specific limits, Taiwan is also scheduled for step-by-step "graduation" from this treatment. In the 1980s, as Taiwan's exports to the United States have continued to rise, and as Taiwan fields more exports, especially some that are technology-intensive, charges of patent infringement and trade mark counterfeiting have also risen.[9] However, these pressures on Taiwan's export community were preceded by the extension of U.S. tariff concessions negotiated with other GATT members in the Tokyo round and under the Generalized Special Preference program. In return, Taiwan has also had to reciprocate with tariff as well as nontariff concessions. All this interaction may in the end have the effect of speeding up the adjustment movement of the Taiwan economy to greater competitiveness, structural adjustment and progressively greater liberalization.

BILATERAL U.S.-ROC TRADE NEGOTIATIONS IN 1978

The center piece of the adjustments of Taiwan's foreign trade system was the bilateral U.S.-ROC trade agreement concluded on December 29, 1978, only two days before the end of formal diplomatic relations between the two countries. Negotiations began in April 1978 and agreement was reached quickly following only five rounds of talks. The U.S. tariff cuts extended to Taiwan under the agreement covered 1,888 items negotiated under GATT's Multilateral Trade Negotiations (MTN) plus 45 additional items in 1979. In return, Taiwan agreed to reduce tariffs on 339 items. The concessions began to take effect by stages as of January 1, 1980, and covered 81.65 percent of U.S. imports from Taiwan (using 1976 as the base year estimate) and 74.23 percent of Taiwan's imports from the United States in the same year.[10]

No less significant were other terms in the agreement which included many NTBs (nontariff barriers), dealing with customs valuation, import licensing, government procurement, counterfeiting, subsidies and countervailing duties, and technical standards for imports.[11] Partly because of the agreement, systematic changes have been made in Taiwan that have eased the flow of imports and, indirectly, exports by removing unncessary irritants between Taiwan and its trading partners.

CUSTOMS SIMPLIFICATIONS AND TARIFF REDUCTIONS

One important adjustment of the trading system has been in the Customs area. It began before August 1971 when Taiwan adopted the Brussels Tariff Nomenclature in commodity classification, increasing the number of items from 1,142 on the old schedule to 3,925 on the new schedule under the BTN divisions,[12] resulting in greater precision in defining the commodities traded. This was followed by annual reviews and revisions of classification, reduction of tariff rate intervals,[13] and, in 1979 and 1982, major rate reductions. In addition, in response to the replacement of fixed exchange rates by floating rates and currency depreciation and price inflation in the world at large, specific rates, followed by compound (specific plus ad valorem) tariffs, were introduced. In 1980, the simple column rates were replaced by a two-column system so that distinction between the general tariff schedule and rates reached by agreement can now be made, thus giving future trade negotiators a much needed legal leeway. Last but not least, the 20 percent addition to invoice value in the valuation of imports to tariff calculations, long in use by ROC customs, has been abolished.

At the end of the 1979 tariff revision, the Customs Administration reported the average import tariff rate at 39.14 percent in comparison with 43.58 percent beforehand. A further downward revision in 1980 lowered the average tariff to 31.19 percent. Additional reductions have been scheduled for the mid-1980s. Underlying these successive tariff reductions has been a shift in economic philosophy and outlook, from treating customs duties primarily as a source of government revenue to using them as a means of negotiating with other nations for promoting both exports and imports. Furthermore, in a period of rising GNP and exports on Taiwan's part in the mid-1980s, tariff reduction and any resultant import expansion can hasten structural change without making sectoral adjustments too difficult in the short run and would therefore be quite opportune.

CUSTOMS DUTIES AS A SOURCE OF REVENUE

In 1965, when U.S. economic aid was terminated, customs duties constituted 22.8 percent of all government revenue, topping all other taxes, and were followed by income from the state monopoly of alcoholic beverages. Personal income tax supplied only 8.95 percent.[14] From fiscal year 1965 through 1978, when the U.S.-ROC bilateral trade talks took place, customs revenue generally accounted for 23-24 percent of the government's income, rising beyond this range to 28 percent only in 1974, probably as a result of the oil price inflation. However, from 1980 onward, available data through 1982 show a steady decline each year of the relative share of customs duties as against a steady increase in that of the personal income tax. In 1982, the share of customs duties in total tax and the alcoholic beverage monopoly revenue had fallen to 16.66 percent while that of income tax had risen to 19.39 percent. The absolute amount of customs revenue actually declined in 1982, which was only the third time it had ever happened since 1954. Although protection of domestic producers continues to be advocated by industry lobbying for higher duties, and the argument is sometimes accepted by the government granting temporary relief to business, a clear trend toward trade liberalization appears to have been set.

LOWERING LICENSING CONTROLS AND DIRECT GOVERNMENT INTERVENTION

Import control has been relaxed and the direct role of the Bureau of Foreign Trade has been reduced in two additional areas. First, Table 6.7 shows how in 1983 Taiwan's foreign trade control system underwent a substantial reclassification of import groups with respect to the types of restrictions applicable. As of September 16, 1983, 25,837 commodity groups or 97.1 percent of the total in the Customs schedule are "permissible imports." Of these, 23,583 or 91.3 percent are without any restriction whatsoever. Special restrictions are applicable to the remaining "permissible imports" but only the 448 groups shown in Table 6.7 are reserved for designated importers, both governmental and private, including, for example, manufacturers, export-processing firms, "large export houses," public enterprises, and so on. Commodities requiring special approvals include insecticides and pharmaceutical items affecting health and environmental quality. Thus virtually all imports have been opened to private business and most are free of government intervention.

Second, while the standardization and reclassification of commodity and tariff schedules by the Customs administration can be dated to 1971, the Board of Foreign Trade, which is responsible for trade policy and its administration, has since September 1970 been shifting the handling of import licensing from itself to the banks. As of the end of 1980, licensing of unrestricted imports could be directly handled by banks, which are designated by the Foreign Exchange Department of the Central Bank, as agents of the Board and without prior reference to it.[15]

In summary, the 1970s and early 1980s witnessed the progressive liberalization of Taiwan's import system. Since export promotion by private business was already an integral part of economic policy, this means the progressive liberalization of all foreign trade. Bilateral trade negotiations with the United States constituted a powerful stimulus at the end of the 1970s. But the process of liberalization began much earlier. The primary motivation was self-generated, stemming from the authorities' conviction that trade is a two-way street and that for a country dependent on trade with the world, such trade cannot rise indefinitely unless imports as well as exports can increase. The economic conditions and policies of other nations must be taken into account.

TABLE 6.7. Reclassification of Commodities for Import Control (number of commodity groups in customs classification)

| | Total | Permissible Imports ||||| Controlled Imports | Prohibited Imports |
		Subject to Special Importer Classifications	Approvals of Designated Government Agencies	Supply Source Restrictions	No Restrictions		
Before 9/16/83	25,664	628	479	1,610	22,947	921	17
After 9/16/83	25,837	448	496	1,310	23,583	751	14
Change	+173	−180	+17	−300	+636	−170	−3

Source: Compiled from Board of Foreign Trade data.

Although the 1979-82 period was one of worldwide recession which also affected Taiwan's principal markets, both merchandise exports and the current account as a whole put in an exemplary performance (except 1980 in the latter case[16]). Apart from the changes in customs practice, the tariff reductions have been accompanied by easing of import licensing and other controls rather than the erection of new nontariff barriers as might well have happened in the absence of a determined policy to liberalize. Trade liberalization has certainly made the Taiwan market generally more accessible to foreign suppliers although time alone will tell how far-reaching the effects will be. So far, liberalization has paid off.

RELAXATION OF EXCHANGE CONTROL

Given the relaxation of trade control it should not be surprising to find simultaneously relaxation of exchange control. In fact, one cannot be strictly enforced without the other. At the end of 1978, when trade liberalization was given a major push, the basic exchange control law also assumed a new look. According to the new regulations, current foreign exchange receipts, including income from exports of goods and services and from investments abroad and other inward remittances, may now be deposited with designated banks in foreign exchange. The depositors are free to make withdrawals in foreign exchange for all business and personal expenses, including foreign travel and family support. Holding of foreign exchange by local residents is legal and such foreign exchange can also be deposited in "foreign exchange deposits" except that deposits made in foreign currency or travellers checks cannot be automatically transferred abroad. The rules governing foreign exchange deposits of this category were last revised in October 1983 after their initial adoption in January 1979 and a first revision in 1981. In effect the gist of the remaining controls is merely to monitor all foreign exchange transactions and to eschew intervention and control by the government except in the case of large transfers of capital for investment or for holding in foreign countries.

Given this increased access to foreign exchange, payments for nontrade purposes are bound to rise. Travel expenditures, family support, and remittances for education abroad all fall into this category. Available data indicate a steady increase in travel expenditure by Taiwan residents since 1978 and in private transfer payments since 1979. Fortunately for Taiwan, the net out-payments on these transactions were, except in 1980, more than offset by the export surplus in goods and services so that the current account continued to be in the black in three out of the four years between 1979 and 1982. However, of the nontrade transactions, travel and private transfer payments plus factor income (investment income and labor income) deserve some further consideration because they touch some very important issues of policy affecting Taiwan's future.

Travel

Until the recent relaxation of foreign exchange control foreign travel purely for pleasure was proscribed. Relaxation of control has come about because the country's balance of payments can now afford such spending and because increasing contact between Taiwan citizens and the rest of the world is deemed beneficial to Taiwan. As a matter of fact, it definitely pays the citizens of a trading nation to have more personal knowledge about people in foreign countries. Some of the travel expense should therefore be better classified as trade-related expenditures. First-hand knowledge about the travel and tour business in foreign countries will also benefit those engaged in tourism for foreigners in Taiwan.

Labor Income

Under "factor income" earnings of Chinese construction workers and engineers in international construction projects have continued through 1982 to yield a small positive balance. As Chinese labor becomes more costly, "upgrading" of such work by using cheaper labor from other countries under the management and design of Taiwan firms points to a future trend. (Korean construction firms in the Middle East have often employed Pakistani and other Asian workers.) Competition may become keener as mainland Chinese workers enter more and more into the field.

Investment Income

Up to 1982, this account has consistently shown a small debit balance in most years; it rose to nearly $200 million in 1981 but fell again to just $40 million in the following year. Although Taiwan's strong international liquidity position would have permitted self-financing of certain large equipment imports purchased on credit, favorable opportunities to borrow which have presented themselves on occasion—such as financing of nuclear power plants—have not been bypassed, on the ground that up to a point foreign indebtedness is a good way to deepen economic relations based on interdependence.

The thought that foreign investment, especially direct investment, may be one of the best ways of acquiring technology has inspired the Taiwan authorities' emphasis on encouraging direct foreign investment both at Hsinchu and elsewhere in Taiwan. More thought probably should be given to investing in firms located abroad that might subsequently establish principal-subsidiary or affiliate relations with counterparts in Taiwan. In this manner, capital export would actually point a way to technology import while conventional thinking links the import of technology with capital import only. Investment in foreign resource production projects—energy and timber reserves and agricultural plantations, for example—constitutes still another approach. Other practices long adopted by Japanese forerunners deserve equally serious assessment and wider appreciation by Taiwan business; these include transfers of existing plants to countries where labor will remain cheaper for some time as new investment for local production gears up for technologies adapted to higher labor cost and automation.

In the long run, Taiwan will undoubtedly be in a much stronger balance of payments position if it can count on positive net balances from investment income. This cannot happen, however, without building up income earning assets abroad either as foreign acquisitions primarily for the sake of technology or as portfolio investments. In the nineteenth century, this used to be accomplished through colonialism and empire building. Today, for small nations like Taiwan, the only way is to develop large current account surpluses through initially an export surplus. This is happening now. (See Table 6.8.)

Private Remittances

Another source of foreign exchange receipts that could be developed for Taiwan and was quite important for China is inward remittance from abroad. Private "unilateral transfers" for family support by

TABLE 6.8. Balances of Taiwan's Current Account and Its Components (million dollars by subaccount)

	Merchandise Trade	Goods and Nonfactor Service	Factor Income	Transfer Payments	Current Account
1965	-66.83	-84.32	-4.85	32.87	-56.30
1973	734.23	569.02	-3.03	0.26	566.25
1974	-830.39	-1,120.60	-4.68	12.63	-1,112.65
1975	-254.50	-580.02	-88.00	7.55	-588.47
1976	684.51	401.64	-132.00	20.32	289.96
1977	1,200.25	973.57	-134.84	4.34	943.07
1978	2,234.51	1,761.62	-63.10	-29.14	1,669.38
1979	1,390.86	434.87	11.13	-221.97	224.03
1980	412.78	-545.64	58.11	-95.08	-698.83
1981	2,081.34	961.90	-261.73	-92.19	607.98
1982	3,693.18	2,440.72	-16.55	-130.99	2,293.18

Source: Council for Economic Planning & Development, Executive Yuan, ROC, *Taiwan Statistical Data Book 1980* and *1983*.

Chinese working overseas, principally in Southeast Asia and North America, were in the 1930s a mainstay in China's balance of payments.[17] Today, in the case of Taiwan, such remittances for family support are not always distinguishable from payments of tuitions and living by the parents of Chinese students who leave Taiwan in thousands each year for studies overseas. The latter remittances, like tourist expenditures, can be regarded as service imports. Alternatively, they can be treated as foreign investment in human resources that could yield "dividend" payments in future family support. In view of the numerous Chinese who have emigrated from Taiwan, including former students who have chosen not to return there for employment, the flow of inward remittances can be enlarged if reasons for keeping up support in Taiwan can be reinforced. A decisive factor is whether family members (especially the parents) of Chinese workers abroad will choose to join the income earners by emigrating or whether they will prefer to stay in Taiwan to be recipients of payments from abroad, at least at some stage of their lives—for example, as children staying with grandparents or as parents of income-earners domiciled abroad, or as retirees collecting foreign pension checks.

106 / BECOMING AN INDUSTRIALIZED NATION

Since 1979 the net debit balance of private transfer payments increased sharply. The figures (in Table 6.8) suggest a greater outflow of payments for family support during 1979-82 than inflow. The remarkable short-run phenomenon is the continued credit balance on current account during most of this period. The real long-run issue is whether the direction of the net flow of transfer payments can be reversed.

DEVELOPING AN INTERNATIONAL FINANCIAL NETWORK

In the past, Taiwan's effort to attract foreign capital has concentrated on direct investment in established industries for production in Taiwan. Innovative policies in the early 1980s have broken new grounds: portfolio investment in Taiwan firms, venture capital in new projects, and offshore banking facilities. At varying stages of implementation, these innovations are meant to propel the Taiwan economy to the center of the international financial nexus.

The Taiwan (ROC) Fund

This is a mutual fund with investments in listed Taiwan companies.[18] The beginning net issue of $41 million was underwritten in October 1983 by nine international banking institutions.[19] The "beneficial certificates" are open for purchase only by nonresidents of Taiwan except those of Japan and, with certain exceptions, of the United States because of certain legal restrictions in both countries. Listing was first sought on the London Stock Exchange. The Fund is managed by the International Investment Trust Company, a joint venture of six ROC banks and one financial and investment firm and the nine foreign underwriters. Capital appreciation is the aim of the Fund.

A Venture Capital Fund

A project still under planning in late 1983 was a venture capital fund to help start high tech firms in Taiwan. As mentioned in Chapter 3, advocates of the fund envisage it as a joint project between Taiwan and foreign investors.

An Offshore Financial Center

The third international financial project is the establishment of offshore banking, similar to the Asian Currency Unit of Singapore, to accept foreign exchange deposits from nonresidents and to make loans to foreign borrowers. As long as official approval is still required for making deposits in or borrowing from a bank located abroad, residents in Taiwan, under the plan now envisaged, would be able to deal with these offshore banks only under the same foreign exchange approval requirements. The offshore units of both domestic and foreign banks operating in the "international financial center" will, however, offer nonresident customers, including those in neighboring countries, a more convenient place to participate in Euro- and Asian dollar (or other currency) markets either as depositors or as borrowers. The usual advantages of higher interests paid on such deposits, on which no local income tax is levied, are higher returns, easy access, and anonymity characteristic of such centers according to the regulations promulgated in December 1983. Taiwan's banking institutions will on their part benefit from wider contacts with foreign financial institutions and expand the scope of their operations, earnings, and experience. The first licenses for offshore operation were issued in June 1984.

Other Institutions in the Offing?

The first two institutions mentioned above are traditional and of the type designed to draw foreign capital into Taiwan. Conceptually, the offshore banking project marks a shift in approach because the role Taiwan's banks will play is that of an intermediary on the world's financial market. Taiwan is not necessarily a principal in the banks' transactions. As a participant in or, in due course, even a leader in international loan syndication, Taiwan's financial houses will begin to derive more income from the business activities of the rest of the world, drawing on the latter's larger financial resources than the Taiwan economy alone has need for or can provide.

A fourth member still missing from the institutional framework being gradually constructed to facilitate the flow of both long- and short-term capital to and from Taiwan should perhaps be contemplated in the not too distant future. That is, a mutual fund of international securities which residents of Taiwan can hold through depository certificates. Conceivably such a fund can be created, and its size regulated from time to time, by allowing it to acquire foreign exchange from the official reserves with NT$ funds obtained from the sale of shares. The foreign exchange will be used to build up the Fund's portfolio of international securities. The size of the Fund can vary with its earnings, as well as periodic purchases of foreign exchange from the official reserve to provide for the eventuality of net redemptions. Once the Fund has come into existence, the authorities can in turn determine how much foreign exchange they wish to put into such portfolio investment according to the country's surplus on current account. Such an additional arrangement can help offset any increase in money supply from unduly large export surpluses while adding to the incentive to export. This would be one additional way of building up foreign assets and future foreign income.

THE EXPANDED CONCEPT OF A REGIONAL TRADE CENTER

Playing the role of an intermediary in merchandise trade is an old concept. Its rudimentary form is transit trade. When goods are imported, repackaged, and re-exported to markets which for one reason or another cannot be conveniently supplied by the original exporters, the transit trade center becomes a wholesale and distribution center. When repackaging graduates into processing, local manufacturing develops. This is a grossly simplified version of the rise of Hong Kong and Singapore as major trade and manufacturing centers in the nineteenth and twentieth centuries. Taiwan's export processing zones have played a similar role. In the 1980s the broadened concept of a regional trade center has gradually emerged.

In this broadened concept goods from Western Europe and the United States would be imported to Taiwan and resold in the first place to Southeast Asian countries. Taiwan would serve as a center not only for redistribution and repackaging, for instance, from large to smaller container ships, but also as a warehouse of spare parts and a provider of after sale service in repair and maintenance.[20] The large pool of skilled technicians in Taiwan and the special training programs in which Dutch and West German firms are already involved offer concrete examples of the basis from which far flung developments are possible. For some manufacturers in Europe and America now competing with Japanese firms at a disadvantage in Southeast Asia on account of distance and the high cost of after sale support in the region this concept offers a way of making Taiwan a regional trade base which no other Western Pacific NIC can provide.

Among the less obvious advantages Taiwan possesses are the special relations the island has with ethnic Chinese communities in the rest of the world,[21] in particular, in the ASEAN member nations and the United States. In regard to the former, the economic prowess of Chinese businessmen in the rapidly developing economies of both Indonesia and Malaysia offers marketing and trading possibilities in the region which can be tied to the technical and economic capabilities of Taiwan.

For those who are familiar with the role of ethnic Chinese business in marketing, finance, and manufacturing in Southeast Asia, it should be easy to imagine how a Southeast Asian sales network can be developed through the joint effort of businessmen in the West, Taiwan, and Southeast Asia and offer effective competition to Japan. In areas where Western technology has an upper hand vis-à-vis Japan but is handicapped by distance and the high cost of expatriate technical personnel working in Asia, the possibility of using Taiwan as a base to compete in Japan's home market itself is another distinct possibility.

There is a long history of educational aid by Taiwan to young ethnic Chinese from Southeast Asia.[22] Many ethnic Chinese engineers and businessmen have received a part of their education and training in Taiwan and have their established contacts there. How these potential, uniquely favorable conditions can be exploited by the West and the ROC presents a challenge to both. In the West, it is well to remember that Japan too can make use of this "Taiwan advantage" and has already done so.

Two Taiwan projects are intimately connected with the above idea. One is a proposal to establish a free trade zone with the usual transit trade, warehousing, and merchandise redistribution aspects. This transit trade emphasis, however, faces three counter-arguments: high infrastructure cost against relatively low returns from transit trade, high future opportunity cost by preempting valuable dock and warehouse space which could find more profitable use later, and security problems. However, if the concepts of high technology, after-sale service and ROC-West cooperation with Southeast Asia

110 / BECOMING AN INDUSTRIALIZED NATION

were grafted onto a pure trade intermediary's role, the weight of the case could be turned. Besides, although the transit trade and regional trade center functions are complementary, they are by no means inseparable.

A second on-going project is the construction of a World Trade Center for staging trade fairs and special trade shows. When completed, this would help make Taiwan a place where people would come to shop, for capital goods to consumer products, including Taiwanese, regional, and Western products. This project broadens the established function of the Council for the Promotion of Foreign Trade which stages trade exhibitions abroad for Taiwan producers and exporters.

POWER POLITICS AND INTERNATIONAL ECONOMICS

Since 1979 a number of innovative measures have been developed by Taiwan to expand the horizon of its financial and trade relations with the rest of the world. It is safe to postulate that much of what has been developed in economic institutions has been to support the broadening of economic relations with other countries and to compensate for the loss of diplomatic relations with many. Absence or loss of diplomatic relations has had its direct as well as indirect adverse economic effects. Most notable among these has been the loss of representation by the ROC on the Boards of the International Monetary Fund and the World Bank. The ROC would not have been ousted from these institutions if the United States had not chosen to help the People's Republic of China expand its international economic standing at the expense of Taiwan.[23] Loss of standing with the IMF and the Bank means that Taiwan can no longer draw on the resources of these institutions should the need for financing either development or the balance of payments arise. Fortunately for Taiwan, none of these financing requirements has arisen.

Among the indirect adverse economic effects of the diplomatic loss have been difficulties for Taiwanese businessmen and for ROC officials in visiting Europe on business and to negotiate on trade and other economic matters, including discrimination against Taiwan. It is only by expanding the economy in spite of these handicaps and by enhancing Taiwan's economic presence and impact that some of the travel problems can de facto be removed. Many of the passport difficulties have been removed as a result, and many other economic contacts—through the establishment of unofficial representation that nevertheless performs most consular functions—have been reestablished. Furthermore, establishment of indirect trade between Taiwan and Eastern Europe has had the effect of opening up tentative channels of a potential dialogue between the ROC and Eastern Europe.

However, political difficulties remain. Among these are excessive dependence on U.S. goodwill which weakens Taiwan's bargaining position in continuing bilateral negotiations, and a theoretically untenable position to agree to the reasonableness of demanding bilateral trade balancing. Lack of assurance on arms purchase has had the effect of making defense spending larger than it might be otherwise and in increasing the sense of insecurity which discourages investment and increases the outflow of capital and trained manpower.

Only by continuing economic growth and by increasing Taiwan's economic impact on the developed countries and the Western Pacific regional powers can the weight of past political loss be pared down further. Trade expansion through commodity upgrading and diversification still point in the right direction. Hence, whatever is necessary to promote these efforts must be accorded top priority.[24]

NOTES

1. Against these outflows of current and capital payments economists very naturally will raise questions about in-payments in similar categories. A question one sometimes hears people raise in Taiwan is whether it is wise to borrow from abroad while owned reserves of foreign monies are rising and perhaps earning a lower rate of interest than the rate one pays.

2. The celebrated case of the United States exporting agricultural products as an illustration of the export of land- and capital-intensive, but not really labor-intensive, products need not detain us here.

3. Report of January 24, 1984.

4. Courtesy of the H.S.I.P. Administration.

5. In absolute value, exports to Japan in 1979 had risen considerably in comparison with the immediately preceding years since 1973; it was at current prices over two and a half times greater than in 1973. See the discussions below.

6. On the issue of the Common Market's discrimination against Taiwan, which is not a GATT member, see Kuo-shu Liang and Ching-ing Hou Liang, "Trade, Technology Transfers, and the Risks of Protectionism: The Experience of the Republic of China," *Industry of Free China* (Taipei), January 1984, Vol. 61, No. 1, pp. 7–22.

7. In the course of U.S.–Taiwan trade negotiations in May 1984, the ROC's Central Bureau of Standards reportedly succeeded in obtaining the recognition

of its accepted standard of approval as an emblem of proven quality for goods produced in Taiwan. *United Daily News* (Taipei), May 21, 1984.

For a thoughtful discussion on patents, trade marks and the protection of monopolies based on technical designs, see Wong, Yi-ting, "Kuo-lai-jen t'an chuan-li yü shang-piao," [Observations on Patents and Trade Marks Based on Experience], *Wei-chien-chi* [Essays of an Observer], (Taipei: Commonwealth Publishing Co., 1984), pp. 191-206.

8. There are exceptions. Two-way trade between Taiwan and the Netherlands reportedly reached $590 million in 1983. *CNA Newsletter* (Taipei: Central News Agency of China), June 1-8, 1984, p. 1.

9. See Subcommittee on Oversight and Investigation of the Committee on Energy and Commerce, U.S. House of Representatives, *Unfair Foreign Trade Practices, Stealing American Intellectual Property: Imitation Is Not Flattery*, 98th Cong., 2nd Sess. (Washington, D.C.: U.S. Government Printing Office, February 1984). According to *The Wall Street Journal*, August 2, 1984, Japan has also lodged complaints about Taiwan on the same ground.

10. Board of Foreign Trade, *Tung-ching Hui-ho Shih-chieh Mo-i T'an-p'an* [The Tokyo Round World Trade Negotiations] (Taipei: January 1980).

11. At the time there were specific U.S. concerns about exports of citrus fruit and passenger cars and permission for American insurance companies to sell insurance in Taiwan.

12. These are divided into 21 sections, 99 chapters and 1,096 headings.

13. In 1974, the tariff classes were first reduced from 45 to 18 and the corresponding ad valorem rates were lowered to a range of zero (exempt) to 100 percent from the former range of zero to 156 percent. Three additional classes of luxury imports (mostly Chinese food products, jewelry and cosmetics) were restored in 1979 and the maximum rate again went back to 156 percent.

14. *Taiwan Statistical Data Book 1983*, pp. 157-158.

15. According to the Board of Foreign Trade, as of August 1984, licenses for 82.34 percent of Taiwan's imports (21,361 commodity groups) can be issued by designated banks; 6.34 percent or 1,646 commodity groups are licensed by the Board itself; 11.32 percent or 2,937 groups require no license. *The World Journal* (San Francisco), July 22, 1984.

16. See the discussion later in this chapter.

17. The traditional "overseas remittances" are comparable to the earnings of present-day construction workers in Saudi Arabia or Indonesia or sailors working on ships. But the latter are short-term workers under contract with foreign entities. The former remittances came from the earnings of individual Chinese who made a living in their own different ways while domiciled in foreign countries.

18. Bonds and money market instruments may also be purchased.

19. The nine underwriters are Credit Suisse, First Boston Ltd., Vickers da Costa Ltd., Robert Fleming & Co. Ltd., Wardley Investment Services, Ltd., Citicorp International Ltd., Gartmore Investment Management Ltd., Lazard Brothers & Co. Ltd., The Nikko Securities Co. (Europe) Ltd., and United Merchant Bank Ltd.

20. Kaohsiung and Taichung were designated as maritime storage and transshipment centers in July 1983 on a one-year trial basis. From July 1983 to April 30, 1984, container transshipment through Kaohsiung reached 360,000 TEU (twenty-foot equivalent units) while the transshipment of bulk cargo at Taichung Harbor came to 1.06 million tons. Compared with the corresponding period before the program, the increases were 267 percent and 103 percent respectively. The harbors of Keelung and Hualien were added to the program in July 1984. *CNA Newsletter*, June 1-8, 1984, p. 7.

21. Wu, Yuan-li and Chun-hsi Wu, *Economic Development in Southeast Asia* (Stanford, CA: Hoover Institution Press, 1980).

22. Ibid.

23. Wu, Yuan-li, "U.S.-ROC (Taiwan) Economic Relations after the 1979 Diplomatic Rupture," in *The American Asian Review* 1, No. 2 (St. John's University, New York: Institute of Asian Studies, 1983), pp. 83-94.

24. Taiwan has the need to find a substitute for Hong Kong which accounted for 7 percent of Taiwan's exports in 1982, its largest single market after the United States and Japan, not to mention various financial and other functions Hong Kong provides on behalf of Taiwan.

7

BEHAVIORAL ACCOMMODATION TO ECONOMIC DEVELOPMENT: PROBING CULTURAL ROOTS

MOTIVES AND ATTITUDES UNDERLYING TAIWAN'S ECONOMIC DEVELOPMENT

If one were to compare Taiwan's economic advance to the progress of a mountain climber, past success has put the person on a plateau: He must now climb farther to reach an even higher elevation. Economic analysis alone can only explain what has made it possible for him to climb so far up; it does not explain what had made him do it.[1] Whatever were the underlying factors, will they continue to prevail or will they diminish as a result of success and increasing economic well-being? Or will the continuation of economic development call for other behavioral traits and psychological resources that were not important before and that may now be found wanting in spite of the favorable characteristics that spurred the population economically before? Unfortunately, given the author's own limitations, it is doubtful that we shall end this chapter with as many answers as there will be questions.

IS THRIFTINESS INBORN?

Some of the major economic reasons for past development in Taiwan were indisputable; one of these was the high savings rate. Past data pointed to increasing savings with rising income but the rate stayed high even after income had risen considerably. Although a substantial part of aggregate savings represented government savings, private savings were high and rising. In the decade of the 1970s, the private sector's marginal propensity to save on an annual basis was at or exceeded 34 percent in five years; it was at or above 25 percent in two other years. It fell below 20 percent in one year (1979) and was negative in another (1975), both times thanks to the oil price hike and its aftermath.[2] The average private propensity to save was invariably close to or above 20 percent and higher than in the previous two decades. Why do people in Taiwan save so much? Might they begin to save a smaller portion of their rising income in the future; might they actually save less absolutely?

One conventional wisdom comes to mind. Inadequate pensions, or their total absence in many employments, have obviously given the working person a real incentive to save for old age and the "rainy day," even at very low levels of income. A second powerful reason for savings, perhaps less obvious to some Western observers today, is to put one's children through increasingly higher levels of education, which rests on the premise that progressive improvement in education is strongly desired. If the sight for such advancement in education is set quite high, obviously the extension of free basic education from six to nine years would not discourage savings by the parents. On the contrary, savings for the children's higher education might even be encouraged by the improved prospect of reaching that goal given a longer tax-supported primary and middle school education. Thus the increasingly better prospects of reaching a higher and higher rung on the educational ladder may act as a positive stimulus to a high marginal propensity to save, as well as a periodically rising savings-income function.[3]

Before one jumps to the conclusion that personal thrift might decline as pensions and social welfare benefits increasingly help provide for old age and the "rainy day," one should ask whether persons in Taiwan who have successfully saved for their old age really dissave during their old age, or save at a substantially lower rate than before? Some Chinese still regard it as "sinful" to draw down whatever inheritance they have received from their forebears. Of those sharing this outlook some would wish to pass an augmented amount to their offspring. If this is true, then those who have saved in their working years will dissave as little as possible during their old age, and the average propensity to save for the population as a whole will not decline with better health and an expanding group of older citizens.

During the first oil crisis in 1974-75, young women who became unemployed on export processing jobs away from home went back to live with their parents. While employed, many young workers would send money home as their contribution to family finances or to help put younger siblings through senior high school or better. Pooling the incomes of family members can help increase family income and savings,[4] which is a habit that has been carried over by Chinese communities overseas. Unlike Western societies, Taiwan may have proportionately fewer young single person households that tend to be always poverty-stricken and are unable to save.

Increasing competition among financial institutions may be desirable as a means of mobilizing savings for investment but can also increase consumption by expanding consumer credit. The advent of credit cards[5] could have the same effect as the habit of seeking instant gratification so characteristic of the consumer-oriented culture of some economically developed societies. This effect must be weighed against the beneficial effect of an expanding domestic market, although increasing consumption can be perfectly compatible even with an increasing rate of savings, if only output and income rise more than proportionately, and savings are used in capital formation. But the possibility that hedonistic behavior as a result of modernization and imitation of the West might have a net adverse effect on savings and undermine the work ethic does exist and is a primary concern of policy makers in another Asian NIC, Singapore. Prime Minister Lee Kuan Yew has sought to counter this potentially pernicious development by introducing Confucian ethic into the school curriculum, sparking thereby a very lively debate.[6]

DEDICATION TO EDUCATION AND THE DRIVE FOR SELF-IMPROVEMENT

As the Taiwan economy developed in the 1960s and 1970s, the pattern of employment changed progressively with the changing economic structure. Farmers became factory workers; producers in declining sectors quickly moved to more promising ones. This signifies several behavioral characteristics, including a willingness to learn new ways and alertness in responding to change. The first trait may be related to the demands many Chinese parents make on their children in educational achievement and to the habit of learning that has been cultivated among the young. Flexibility and adaptability make for higher employment—and shorter unemployment—if the world market for one's products is a fickle one.

But why have people in Taiwan been so flexible and adaptable in the past? Is there an innate capacity always to strive for success, or is it born of fear lest in a highly competitive society and hostile world one might not be able to survive? If high tech is to dominate Taiwan's future, increasing specialization and longer educational preparations will require continuing education for workers at all levels. Will Taiwan's future workers, both young and old, continue to maintain the attitude toward education and the work ethic with it that they now try to inculcate in their children? Thus far the labor force in Taiwan does not seem to have lost its desire for self-improvement, but will the next generation be endowed with the same drive if the present generation proves as successful in continuing the economic advance as it hopes to be?

Many a Chinese proverb attempts to summarize what is believed to be true empirically in Chinese history. According to one such saying, the rich family of a person of humble beginnings who makes his fortune during his own lifetime is likely to return to its initial state of poverty in the third generation. This is meant to say that work ethic and personal drive will be lost after a lifetime of affluence in the second generation and as a result of the upbringing of the third generation, if not already of the second. However, for the society as a whole, this need not be true if enough upward and lateral mobility always manages to bring up new members in the leading échelons and sectors of the society. Although definitive findings are not immediately available, some recent studies suggest that a high degree of upward and lateral mobility does exist in Taiwan and should exert an offsetting influence on any tendency for the drive for self-improvement to decline in the society as a whole.[7]

FROM STRONG COMPETITIVENESS TO UNFAIR COMPETITION

To be quick in entering another person's new-found profitable field is only second to being in the field first. Buyers for large Western mercantile firms who visit Taiwan are quickly besieged by local exporters and manufacturers offering to sell or to make on order what is in demand, each trying to outdo the next. Such alacrity and competitiveness are a classic illustration of a high degree, some might say an exaggerated degree, of freedom of entry that impacts on profit and price and rebounds to the benefit of the buyer. This is all to the good if competing producers are kept on their toes and consumers, whether foreign or domestic, are benefited. But there can also be adverse effects.

Individual firms facing cut-throat competition are less likely to make long-term plans. They are more prone to having a very short planning horizon, and are thus unlikely to pursue any given undertaking on a really long-run basis. This has the same negative effect on making new long-term investments and long-range R&D efforts as would any heightened sense of insecurity about the future which can arise for many other reasons.

A short planning horizon can make people worry much less about "legal niceties" such as the property rights of others—for example, using other people's trademarks, patents—or about the external costs one incurs on specific third parties, or about the social cost one inflicts on the society as a whole which, in the long run, would include oneself. If the rules of competition are not clearly laid down and observed by all, the marketplace can become a jungle and continuing growth of the economy as a whole would be well-nigh impossible. Counterfeiting, which has been a sore point between Taiwan and the United States, is by no means suffered by American sellers only. Producers in Taiwan are more frequently victims of ruthless competitors among their own countrymen.

On the one hand, abstracting from the legal aspect, in cases where the imitation or outright copying of another firm's product entails considerable effort on the part of the copier, it presupposes substantial technical ability on the latter's part. This can be regarded actually as evidence of successful, though unintentional technology transfer. Successful technological upgrading has generally gone through a sequence of imitation, adaptation (especially for greater, related commercial uses), and innovation. The experience of Japan testifies to this. On the other hand, when counterfeiting becomes an international issue and threatens to damage the good name of all exporters from Taiwan and to invite retaliation against all Taiwan exports, the social irresponsibility of the act, over and above its illegality, becomes one of many similar obstacles to continuing economic development.

PAYING FOR EXTERNAL COSTS AND TAKING A "FREE RIDE"

The electronic industry, which is one of Taiwan's strategic developing industries, and other industries new to Taiwan can become sources of environmental pollution, as has been shown in California, often in ways not known before. Removal of the possible pollutants either by prevention or by corrective measures entails a cost that should be recognized and borne by the perpetrator. As another example, the expansion of a particular business may lead to local traffic congestion—a fact well known to many Taiwan commuters—and result in greater demand on road building and maintenance for which the government budget and, ultimately, the taxpayers must pay. Taiwan is by no means the solitary source of examples of unintentional as well as purposeful avoidance by individual businesses to pay for social costs, or to pay for benefits received from the public sector that are shared by other beneficiaries. Such cases and their importance are likely to multiply as the economy develops further. There are both domestic and international ramifications.

It should be pointed out that critics in Taiwan are quite severe on themselves in this regard. Writing in the January, 1984 volume of *Industry of Free China*,[8] a prominent economic planner and administrator thought that while some people in Taiwan would like to be left totally alone by society to manage their own affairs, they acted as if the government should take care of everything else outside their own door—the roads, the public utilities, law and order, and all other public services, without either their participation or their sharing of the cost. Similarly, a questionnaire survey conducted by the Ministry of Education[9] in conjunction with the Prime Minister's Office reported in early 1984 that when students were asked to rank four qualities that they thought needed strengthening most among their contemporaries—patriotism, concern for the public's well-being, personal drive, and self-confidence—their answers were close to being unanimous. (See Table 7.1.) The student samples were taken from the junior high school up through the senior high school, senior vocational school, junior college, college, and university levels. The top answer was either patriotism or concern for the public's well-being. These are qualities that are regarded as most needing reinforcement. Except at the high school level, where the younger set apparently saw the need for more self-confidence, the self-perception of Taiwan's

TABLE 7.1. Ranking of Personal Qualities Requiring Reinforcement in Taiwan's Youth as Perceived by Students

Academic Level Students in the Sample*	First Patriotism	Second Concern for the Public's Well-being	Third Personal Drive	Fourth Self-Confidence
Junior high school	1	2	4	3
Senior high school	2	1	4	3
Senior vocational high school	2	1	4	3
Junior college and polytechnics	2	1	3	4
University or college	2	1	3	4

*The sample includes (1) 20 universities, colleges and junior colleges (and polytechnics), (2) 10 senior high schools, (3) 10 senior vocational schools, and (4) 20 junior high schools. The numbers of students samples were (1) 2,188, (2) 983, (3) 1,034, and (4) 2,760 respectively, including both males and females.
Source: China Forum (Taipei), January 1984, Vol. 11, No. 1, pp. 11-52 (see Note 9).

youth would seem to coincide with the mature lament of many a policy maker. The survey in question was intended as an evaluation for the guidance of the nation's civic education program. The implications of the answers to the questionnaires are unmistakable. They offer both a social comment and an enormous positive opportunity, for those who need attitudinal reinforcement have obviously perceived the need themselves.

Some of the new institutions designed to make Taiwan's economic system more efficient and conducive to continuing development will offer new personal and business opportunities that can also be misused by persons lacking scruples. For instance, a more active securities market could lead to insider trading that undermines its credibility as a marketplace for investors and savers. The beneficial effect of a credit-rating system could be nullified by falsified financial reports. The development of new channels of raising capital may be matched by equally ingenious methods of defrauding the unsuspecting public. The successful launching of new products by manufacturers and their advertisers increases the demand on safeguarding professional quality standards[10] and truth in representation. The faster the rate of economic development from the high level the Taiwan economy has already set, the greater is the opportunity for wrongdoing and the more urgent will be the need for a judicious mixture of law and ethics.

DEPENDENCY ON THE GOVERNMENT?

A short planning horizon reduces the businessman's propensity for risk taking over the long run. One tends to reduce spending on long-term R&D to a minimum and to wait for the government to provide the initiative, funding, and leadership. The short view also discourages efforts to diversify export markets where large expenditures on a sustained basis are required. This in turn forces the government, which correctly sees these undertakings as indispensable, to be much more activist and interventionist than it probably should be and many policy makers wish it to be. Since an activist government is likely to make mistakes, and since it is bound to make demands on the business community and the public, the latter may then complain about government over-regulation. If competition within a well-defined legal order is to take place and plans of future economic development, including R&D, investment, foreign market development, and manpower training are all to be based on long-run considerations, both private business and government agencies must be willing to take risks, make honest mistakes, and over the long run, minimize such mistakes by becoming more knowledgeable and more deliberate and thus reap collectively the benefit of continuing growth.

Acceptance of the following propositions, it seems, has to be seriously contemplated if the new institutions and policies for continuing growth are to be properly matched with appropriate attitudes and behaviors:

First, since the Taiwan economy has progressed so far and so fast on the basis of private entrepreneurship and initiative, private efforts will remain the principal engine of growth. However, in view of the growing complexity of technology, institutions, and international in addition to domestic involvement of many more persons and businesses, there must be a greater real concern about third party, and the society's collective, interests on the part of individuals and private business.

Second, since private business is by definition out to make profit and the ROC government's policy is to promote economic growth through the efforts of private business, it does not have to shy away from adopting policies that benefit business in general. This too may require a re-examination of conventional attitudes and presumptions of what constitutes ethical and legal behavior.[11]

ECONOMIC DEVELOPMENT AND THE CONFUCIAN ETHIC

The pattern of human behavior is by no means static and adaptation to the environment is known to induce adjustment. However, if the cultural heritage and value system that play a determining role in the majority's behavior are long-standing, adjustment, even if forthcoming, will be slow. Therefore, the relevant question about Taiwan in the first place is not how business and individual behavior might in time change, but whether the existing behavioral pattern is or can be quickly adjusted to be conducive to the efficient functioning of new and old economic institutions and policies. Since the residents on Taiwan are predominantly Chinese, the question becomes one on the impact of the dominant influence of Confucian ethics on economic development.

The answer to this question is surprisingly complex and Singapore's open campaign to introduce a Confucian ethics course in the island republic's school system has curiously confused the matter somewhat. In the Singapore case, there are several conflicting public concerns about the introduction of Confucian ethics in the schools' curriculum. Of these, two in particular are relevant in the present connection. On the one hand, Confucian ethics is regarded as a counterweight to hedonism, decline of productivity, and unethical behavior by encouraging work, thrift, thirst for knowledge, and the cultivation of virtuous personal conduct. On the other hand, there are those who see in Confucian emphasis on the family, its conservative approach to change, and even personal modesty, thrift, and disapproval of conspicuous consumption the roots of nepotism, limitation of business expansion, loss of competitiveness, and slowing of modernization and expansion of the market. Each of these arguments can be supported by the selective use of empirical data so that the critical issue really has to do with the practical and selective application of Confucianism and whether Confucian ethics truly constitute a driving force in Sinic societies like Singapore, Hong Kong, and, in the present case, Taiwan.

The ranks of economic policy makers and academicians in Taiwan interested in the relationship of the behavior of individuals and business to economic development seem to be slowly expanding.[12] Worried about the appropriate coordination of behavioral and institutional changes, they have in particular questioned the cultural roots of irresponsible social behavior and the alleged adverse impact of Confucian teaching on the drive for economic development.

FROM CONFUCIAN SELF-CULTIVATION TO SOCIAL RESPONSIBILITY[13]

Family cohesiveness can be a great help to individuals facing hostile conditions. Mention has been made earlier of the role played by such cohesiveness in Taiwan during the 1974–75 oil crisis. Family cohesiveness has also been a help to the development of business relations between Hong Kong Chinese and the ethnic Chinese community in Southeast Asian countries. In countries where anti-Chinese sentiments were high, survival of local Chinese businesses was made possible partly as a result of cooperation and loyalty of family members to one another. Yet misuse of family connections can be damaging to corporate expansion and result in inefficiency and poor business performance. The net effect of emphasis on the family obviously depends upon their concomitant circumstances, and it certainly is a misinterpretation of Confucian ethics to equate emphasis on the family to lack of social responsibility.

Conceptually, the true Confucian has always called for the extension of what one should do for one's family to the nation, and ultimately to the world. The family is not the end of the Confucian ethical scheme; it is only the beginning. It is the first step in the expansion of the self-cultivation process of the individual,[14] from self to the family, to the nation, and, finally to the world. Self-cultivation is not the pursuit of selfish interests but the cultivation of oneself as a moral person, not excluding the pursuit of one's own interest. Granted that the expansion of a person's horizon with respect to social obligation becomes increasingly less automatic as one leaves the circle of one's immediate family and friends, Confucian ethic certainly does not stop its concern at the family's threshold.

A related issue concerns the rule of law in economic relations. This issue has been highlighted in recent discussions in Taiwan on social behavior and interpersonal relationships in connection with trademark counterfeiting, patent invasions, fraudulent bankruptcies, and flights of businessmen with other people's funds. It has been pointed out that the five traditional principal interpersonal relationships that are governed by generally accepted standards of behavior are relationships between persons known to one another. The five relations are between the sovereign and the subject (or, in the modern version, between the state and the citizen), between parents and children, between husband and wife, between siblings, and between friends. Even in the first case, the sovereign would certainly be identifiable in the mind of the subject. However, since no special mention is made of a person's relationship to other persons who are unknown to him or who are not readily identifiable, the individual lacks a sense of responsibility toward the amorphous public and toward individual strangers. It is argued, therefore, that as an economy develops in size, commercialization beyond the small enterprise level often leads to serious problems (1) of business ethics and rules of competition, and (2) involving "public goods," "free riders," and "externalities." Actually, here again one needs to be reminded that not only does Confucian ethic stipulate that the stranger should be treated with the same faithfulness and consideration as a friend, but all the problems inherent in business ethics and in externalities are taken care of in the Confucian golden rule: "Do not do unto others what you would not wish others to do unto you." If one does not wish to suffer from environmental pollution perpetrated by others, whether deliberately or unwittingly, it behooves one not to ride free oneself. Furthermore, according to Confucian teaching, the person of virtue ought to be second to none when confronted with an opportunity to do good, which is of course the essence of voluntarism. This could be interpreted as a call to produce even at one's own cost a public good beneficial to all. (*Chün-tzu tang jen pu rang.*) The growth of Chinese overseas remittance business in Southeast Asia in the past and the highly developed domestic banking system of China were all founded on ethical behavior among strangers. Among Chinese businessmen in the past the spoken word was as good as a written contract.

INTERNALIZING SANCTIONS AS A COMPLEMENT TO THE RULE OF LAW

As for the rule of law under which fair competition can be practiced by all who participate in the market, the Confucian ethic calls for the internalization of sanctions. The code of behavior (*li*) and the acceptance of one's moral obligation unto oneself in dealing with others (*yi*) are a major part of the Confucian ideal. The more an individual or a business conducts itself according to a moral code and strictly observed standards, the less will it be necessary to formalize sanctions through legally enforceable laws. This does not mean that laws governing market behavior and property rights can be dispensed with, for there will always be persons who are lax in self-restraint, but it does mean that the more acceptable behavior and fair play are internalized, the less will be the need for an overweening government with its courts and regulatory agencies. A less burdensome and more limited governance will create a freer environment favorable to enterprise. Between Confucians and legalists, the Chinese cultural tradition can readily accommodate both just as an equilibrium can be struck between law and self-discipline although modern societies in the West have generally put more faith in law, at the cost perhaps of more litigation, and sometimes less justice, than necessary.

KNOWLEDGE AND REASON UNDERLYING ECONOMIC PROGRESS AND FREEDOM

The internalization of sanctions or self-restraint is never conceived as inborn although individuals are regarded by Confucians as educable. Both the thirst for knowledge and the inculcation of moral behavior are to be satisfied through education which in the Confucian tradition is a life-long occupation. To the true Confucian, education must not only cater to the intellect, it must also offer guidance on moral behavior, which is only a reasonable requirement for social harmony and a nonfractious social order. Hence, in conventional economic terms, Confucian ethic favors optimization only when externalities in the broad sense are fully taken into account. Knowledge and reason constitute an antithesis to any stifling totalitarian ideology, be it monarchist or communist, or the doctrine of the centralist planner in the economic sphere. Besides, only moral persons who restrain their own venal appetites qualify as leaders. No dictators therefore would qualify according to this Confucian criterion.

Contrary to the fears of some businessmen in Singapore, Confucianism is not at all inimical to business or Schumpeterian entrepreneurs. Not only has Confucius' own admiration and approval of his businessman-disciple Tze-kung been frequently cited as proof of this point, but Confucians and legalists both share the belief that only when living standards have reached a certain level will it be possible to educate the citizenry on right and wrong and expect full compliance. That carefully designed legislation strictly enforced is a necessary complement goes, however, without saying. The Taiwan economy has clearly reached this stage.

If the attitude of the younger generation revealed by the Ministry of Education's poll is correct. Taiwan's youth are more than ready for moral guidance and social responsibility. Where then are the educators? Whose role is it? One would surmise that this role must be shared by policy makers, professional educators and academicians, the communications media and publicists, and, last but by no means the least, business leaders and members of the public themselves. Enlightened and thoughtful businessmen in Taiwan have themselves said so. It is a social education movement that none need wait for others to begin.

ATTITUDINAL CHANGE AND EXTENDING THE PLANNING HORIZON

The Confucian way in its modernized form draws on past Chinese traditions, which should reduce resistance to its propagation, but it requires adjustments in individual as well as business behavior. It extends well beyond those few conventionally identified virtues which have made possible the rapid economic development in the past of Taiwan and other Asian NICs. Traditional growth-inducing factors like the work ethic, thrift, and enterprise are still necessary but they are no longer sufficient to sustain economic progress in Taiwan indefinitely by themselves. What is needed to sustain growth is a special application of the enterprising spirit that will focus the country's psychological resources on continuing development through the advancement of knowledge and its application, together with the necessary institutional and behavioral adjustments, the last corresponding to what the true Confucian would call self-cultivation.

A strong motivation must be supplied, and that obviously cannot be limited to continuing improvements in material well-being as measured, say, by GNP per capita. A progressively more satisfying way of life in freedom, for an increasingly larger majority of the population, that is well worth working harder than one does now to achieve, and continuing to work hard to protect, can perhaps provide a common goal to replace the struggle for economic and physical survival that has been the powerful incentive in the past for all the Asian NICs. This concept is more comprehensive than "quality of life." It is what would make those who leave Taiwan for study or work elsewhere wish to return for extended visits or long-term residence. It is what would make Chinese parents resident abroad send their children to Taiwan during at least a part of the latter's formative years for some of their education. It is what would make people wish to spend some of their own retirement years in Taiwan or to see their own parents retire there. It is what makes those who invest in other countries for good economic reasons also wish to invest in Taiwan. It is what makes people send money to Taiwan for personal as well as business purposes.

If Taiwan were to attain this hypothetical state, the vision of "brain drain" would disappear. In its place the outflow of human capital would be met by a reverse flow both of returns on prior human investments abroad and of initial inflows of human capital into Taiwan. The same would be true for nonhuman capital. Given such a vision and the determination to make it a reality, who is to say that the goal cannot be accomplished.

A POSTSCRIPT

The way to continuing economic development charted for the Taiwan economy by the country's policy makers is still being tested. No full assessment of the strategy for changing the economic structure in favor of the knowledge-intensive industries and with growing internationalization can be made until a few more years from now.

In the meantime, since the outcome of the Taiwan strategy has been relatively successful so far, what can we say of its transferability to other countries? Without attempting to answer this question immediately, we can ask several more questions preliminary to answering the first one.

First, if we are also dealing with a country where the relatively scant supply of natural resources is comparable to that of Taiwan, the first question needing an answer is whether the country possesses a high propensity to save, a strong work ethic, and considerable business acumen?

Second, for moving to a more fundamental change in the economic structure towards the more knowledge-intensive sectors, the key question to be answered must be the state of the educational infrastructure and the possibility of expanding higher education for the primary purpose of broadening applied research and development and the commercialization of innovations, not for the purpose of producing an intellectual elite, which too many of the few universities in LDCs try to do.

The third question must be whether tradition and vested interests would preclude changes in the economic structure and in institutions that can help mobilize domestic and foreign resources for continuing development and help pay for the use of foreign resources without creating large balance of payments difficulties in the future.

Finally, the existence of an appropriate behavioral pattern must be assured. If no such cultural flexibility exists at the given time, whether it can be changed peacefully and at a reasonable pace will hold the key.

But even a more basic question must be raised before all those we have listed. Since the conditions in each country vary and the specific circumstances must be considered in raising and resolving the above issues, there must be in control policy makers who know how and when to find answers for each of these questions. The political system must be such as to put such persons in a policy-making position. Unless this condition is present, one can hardly expect the right questions to be asked at the appropriate time, still less to have the right answers.

If the country in question is rich in natural resources, this may reduce the scale of domestic savings required. It may also lower the demand for foreign exchange from other sources than resource exports and reduce a potential balance of payments problem.[15] However, the same set of questions must still be asked and answered, and one is tempted to think that there are perhaps fewer real differences between the resource-rich and the resource-poor countries in their comparative prospects for continuing development than one might be led to believe except that a resource-rich country can probably have more chances to try if it fails at first.

NOTES

1. For some incisive comments on conventional economic explanations of Taiwan's past performance see H. J. Duller, *The Socio-cultural Context of Taiwan's Economic Development* (Taipei: Institute of the Three Principles of the People, November 1983), Papers in Social Sciences, No. 83–85.

2. See the Council for Economic Planning and Development, *Taiwan Statistical Data Book 1981* (Taipei, 1981), Tables 3–13, p. 52.

3. This and other seemingly plausible—that is, to this author—hypotheses can perhaps be tested in Taiwan's expanding institutions of applied economics and survey research if they have not already been tested.

4. See, for instance, Yuan-li Wu, ed., *The Economic Condition of Chinese Americans* (Chicago: Pacific/Asian American Mental Health Research Center, 1980).

5. A United Debit (N.B. *not credit*) Card Center was inaugurated in June 1984 by seven domestic financial institutions in Taiwan to replace credit cards issued previously by individual investment and trust companies. (*CNA News Features* report by Lillian Liu (Taipei), June 1984, No. 4.) Perhaps going on credit card spending sprees can be discouraged by calling it a debit card and imposing income and bank balance requirements as seems to be the case in Taiwan. The participating banks have reportedly set the monthly spending limit of each cardholder at between 5 and 20 percent of the person's annual income.

6. Lü, Wu-chi, "Hsin-chia-p'o ti Ru-chia Lun-li Chiao-yü [Education in Confucian Ethics in Singapore], in *Chung-kuo Lun-t'an* [China Forum] (Taipei), Vol. 18, No. 3, May 10, 1984, pp. 56–59. Readers interested in this subject can consult the Singapore press of 1982–83.

7. See Hsü, Chia-yu, "Ch'u-shen Yü Ch'eng-chiu: Taiwan Ti-chü ti Shih-cheng Yen-chiu" [Origin and Achievement: An Empirical Study in Taiwan], *Essays on the Integration of Social Sciences* (Taipei: Institute of the Three Principles of the People, August 1982), Monograph Series edited by Chau-nan Chen, Yu-lung Kiang, and Kuanjeng Chen, No. 9, pp. 265–299.

8. Wang, Chang-ch'ing, "Ching-chi Chien-she yü Shen-ho Shu-chih" [Economic Development and the Quality of Life], in *Industry of Free China* (Taipei: Council for Economic Planning and Development), January 1984, Vol. 51, No. 1, pp. 1–5.

9. Ch'eng, Yün, "Chia-yü-pu Shih-shih, 'Chia-ch'iang T'uei-chan Chi'ing-shao-nien Kung-min Chiao-yü Chi-hua' Wen-chüan Tiao-ch'a Pao-kao Tsai-yao" [Abstract from the Ministry of Education's Survey Report on "Plans to Expand Civic Education among the Young"], in *China Forum* (Taipei), January 1984, Vol. 11, No. 1, pp. 10–52.

10. Taiwan's Bureau of Standards has been trying to introduce such officially approved logos of quality certifications for the export trade. *United Daily News*, Overseas Edition (Taipei), May 21, 1984.

11. The above propositions in no way ignore the importance of policy concerns about national security and distributive equity, both being preconditions of political stability and economic development. A great deal of writing has already appeared in Taiwan on the effect on income distribution of changes in the economic structure and technology. For samples of this literature see, for instance, the essays in the *Proceedings of the July 1978 Conference on Income Distribution* sponsored by the Institute of Economics, Academia Sinica. Also Chu and Tsaur, referred to in Chapter 1, Note 10; and Paul K. C. Liu's works, including "Technological Progress, Economic Structure and Income Distribution in Taiwan." *Paper presented to the ASPAC Conference* at Fairbanks, Alaska, June 1983.

12. See, for instance, Wong Yi-ting, *Wei-k'an-chi* [Chirps Close to the Threshold–Collected Essays] 1984. Also, Sun Chen, "She-hui, Ching-chi yü K'o-chi Fa'chan" [Society, the Economy and S&T Development]. Paper presented to *the Seminar on Society, Culture and S&T Development*, Taipei, August 24, 1983; and K. T. Li, who has been prolific on this subject in "ROC's Position and Role in Current International Economic Relations," in *Industry of Free China* (Taipei), January 1984, Vol. 61, No. 1, pp. 1-6. See also, Sun Chen's article on education in the *United Daily News*, January 1, 1983, and an interview of Sun in the same newspaper on December 22, 1982.

13. These views were presented by the author to a group discussion on Sinic culture and the Asian NICs at the 1983 Santa Barbara, California meeting of the American Association for Chinese Studies.

14. Self-cultivation is not self-indulgence and promotion of selfish interest but the cultivation of a moral and rational being. Making a living is of course a part of life and is not insulated from the process of self-cultivation.

15. This statement is quite arguable in the light of the experience of the debt-ridden resource-exporting developing countries in the early 1980s.

INDEX

INDEX

Aeronautical engineering, 45
agriculture, 23, 25, 28, 40, 49-50;
   agricultural exports, 89, 92;
   credit for, 59-60
anti-poverty program, 6-7
Argentina, 2
ASEAN, 91, 109
Asian Development Bank (ADB), 5
automation, 47, 49

Balance of payments, 87, 104;
   see also current account
Bank of China, 60
Bank of Communications, 30, 59-60
banker's acceptances, 55
Belgium, 90, 93, 96
biological engineering, 45, 47
Brazil, 2
Britain, 49, 90, 92-94, 96
BTN (Brussels Tariff Nomenclature), 98
budget, balancing of, 23, 35; educational, 77-80; revenue sources, 99, 100
Bureau of Vocational Training, 72, 83

Capital export, 15, 67, 103, 104-05, 107-08
capital formation, gross fixed, 10; inventory, 10; share of manufacturing, 12; *see also* investment
capital movement, 17, 127
Carter, Jimmy, 23
capital market, access to, 17; *see also* banks

Central Bank, the, 8, 32, 34, 60, 100
Central Trust of China, 59
Chao, Y. T. (Yao-tung), 28-29
Chiang Ching-kuo, 23, 25
Chiaotung University, 42
China Air Lines, 27
Chiu, Paul C. H., 55
Chou Enlai (*also* Zhou Enlai), 3
Chung-hua Institution for Economic Research, 34
commercial banks, 25, 56-59, 60, 100
commercial papers, 55, 56
Commission of Assistance to Young Chinese; *see* National Youth Commission
Common Market; *see* European market
comparative advantage, 22, 26, 28, 45-46
computer; *see* information industry
Confucian ethics; *see* ethical standards
container shipping, 27
Cooperative Bank of Taiwan, 59
Council for Economic Planning and Development, 2, 13, 82, 80-81, 82, 89
Council for the Promotion of Foreign Trade, 109
counterfeiting, 118, 124
credit cards, 62, 116
credit rating, 62
curb market, 60
currency, 55
current account, 11, 15, 100, 103-06, 107-08
customs, 98-100

133

Defense effort, 7, 46
deposits, demand, 55; savings, 55; time, 55
depreciation, accelerated, 63
Development Fund, 60, 63, 67

Eastern Europe, 111
education, 17, 25, 32, 45, 80-83; graduate, 76, 80; international, 87; junior colleges (polytechnics), 74, 78, 80; moral, 125; on Europe, 87; primary and junior high school, 74-75; relationship to saving, 115; school age children in school, 75; senior high school, 74; student attitude, 119-20; student-teacher ratio, 75; university and college, 74-77, 80
Education, Ministry of, 72, 75, 119, 126
Economic Affairs, Ministry of, 72
electrical machinery, 89
electronics, 45, 49, 90, 118
emigration, 87, 105
employment, agricultural, 13; non-agricultural, 13
energy, 46-47
equity, 6, 19, 28, 35, 62
equity-debt ratio, 33, 56
ethical standards, 120, 122-25; and rule of law, 123, 125
European market, 90-95
exchange control liberalization, 102
exchange rate, 35, 98
Export-Import Bank of China, 59
exports, benefits from GSP, 96; commodity composition, 14-15, 89; diversification of, 15, 92; factor service, 15; foreign capital, role of, 12; growth, 5, 18, 89; importance of, 5; income elasticity of demand, 5; marketing, 12, 94; product identification, 92; ratio to GNP, 11, 14, 18; share in GNP, 5; share in industrial products, 12; surplus, 5, 11; talent, 83

Factor service, export of, 15, 17, 103-05
Farmers' Bank of China, 59
financial assets, access to, 53-54, 57-58
financial policy, banking control, 30; tariffs, 30; tax policy, 30, 35; use of government assets, 30
fiscal policy, 35; *see also* financial policy
fishing, 49, 50; credit for, 59
food industry research institute, 42
food technology, 47
foreign banks, 94, 106
foreign capital, demonstration effect, 12; export marketing, 12; investment in Hsinchu S.I.P., 48-49; ratio in capital formation, 12; technology import, 15, 39-40, 45, 67; versus domestic capital, 29
foreign debt, 103; service (ratio), 12
foreign exchange deposits, 102
foreign investment; *see* foreign capital
Foreign Trade, Board of, 100; policy, 23-24, 87, 97-102, 108-09
foreign travel, 103
France, 90, 93, 96
free trade zone, 109
fruit planting, *see* agriculture

GATT, 97
GDP, *see* gross domestic product

GNP, *see* gross national product
gross domestic product, growth rate, 1; real GDP, 2
gross national product, and education expenditure, 77-80; export/GNP ratio, 11, 18; growth rate, 7, 9, 18; import/GNP ratio, 18; investment ratio, 10, 18; per capita, 1, 2, 9, 54; savings ratio, 10, 18, 54, 115

Holland, 83, 90, 96, 109
Hong Kong, business behavior, 123; competition with Taiwan, 5, 92; GDG growth rate, 2; GNP per capita, 2; investment in Hsinchu, 49; market, 91; regional economic role, 87, 108
horticulture, *see* agriculture
household savings, 55
Hsin-chu, 41-42, 44, 45, 90, 104; *see also* Science-based Industry Park
Hsü Li-teh, 30-31
human capital, *see* human resource
human resource, 42-45, 47, 84, 105, 127; demand and supply in engineering and science, 43

Import licensing, 100
imports, 5, 18, 88, 100; ratio to GNP, 11, 14, 18; talent, 83
income elasticity: of demand for money, 35
income tax, 99-100, 107
Indonesia, 15, 90, 109
industrial market economics, 2
industrial exports, 89
industrial policy, 23-28; scale, 29
inflation, 34, 35
information industry, 26, 30, 45, 49, 90
interest rate, 7, 34, 35, 62-63
International Monetary Fund, 5, 12, 110
internationalization, 15, 17, 31, 36, 86, 106-10; *see also* liberalization of trade
investment: abroad, 87; gross domestic, 65; in infrastructure, 23; inducements of, 25
Italy, 90, 93, 96

Japan, Asian Development Bank, policy to seat PRC, 5; bank loans in, 56; GDP growth rate, 2; GNP per capita, 2; imports from Taiwan, 94; investment trust regulation, 66; market in, 90, 93, 109; portfolio investment in Taiwan, 106; Western competition with, 109

Kaohsiung, 27
knowledge-intensive industry, 39-40, 45-46; staffing and wage scale, 44
Korea, competiton with Taiwan, 5, 92, 103; debt service ratio, 2; GDP growth rate, 2; GNP per capita, 2; investment trust regulation, 66; trade with Taiwan, 92; truce, 3
Ku Cheng-fu, 32
Kuomintang, *see* Nationalist Party
Kuwait, 92

Labor mobility, 70-71
labor productivity in manufacturing, 16, 18
Land Bank of Taiwan, 59-60
land reform, 6
land rent, 42
large trading companies, 24
laser, 47
LDC, 1, 3, 7, 14, 27, 45, 64, 128
Lee Kuan Yew, 116
less developed countries, *see* LDC
liberalization of trade, *see* foreign trade policy
loans and discounts, 57
London Stock Exchange, 106

Machine exports, 90
Malaysia, 90, 109
manpower, 17, 25-26, 72, 80-83
manufacturing, firms, 65; production, 18, productivity, 18
Mao Tse-tung (*also* Mao Zedong), 6
middle income nations, 1, 2, 9
Medium and Small Business Bank of Taiwan, 59-60
mobility of labor, 117-18
monetary policy, 7, 33-34, 61
MTN (multilateral trade negotiations), 97

National Science Council, 42, 45, 72
National Youth Commission, 45, 72
Nationalist Party, 6
net domestic product, agricultural, 13; nonagricultural, 13
newly industrializing countries, 1, 26, 87, 109, 116, 127
NIC, *see* newly industrializing countries
Nixon, Richard, 3

nonprofit organizations, 55-56
NTBs (nontariff barriers), 98

OECD, 66
offshore banking, 107
oil, price hike, effect of, 3, 5, 8, 9, 23, 115
OPEC, 1, 89; oil price, 1
Organization of Petroleum Exporting Countries, *see* OPEC

Pensions for old age, 115
People's Republic of China, *see* PRC
Philippines, 90
pollution, 45-46
population, 18
Postal Remittance, Directorate of, 59-60
PRC, emulation of Taiwan, 27; GDP growth rate, 2; GNP per capita, 2; psychological warfare, 4, 6, 92; UN seat, 3
precision equipment, 45, 49
price, stability, 7-8, 23, 35
private sector, relation with government, 121-22; social responsibility, 32, 80, 118-19; structural change, 32, 46, 62-63
product life style, 46
production, agricultural, 18; industrial, 18
protection, against Taiwan exports, 5, 15, 92, 97; undesirable, 15, 29, 36
public accounting, 64

Quality of Life, 127

R&D, 17, 25, 36, 40, 47, 49-51, 71, 72, 80
real wage rate, 15
remittances from abroad, *see* unilateral transfers
re-unification, 6
Republic of China, economic equality, 6-7, 19, 28; financial policy, 30-31, 62; ideology, 6; inflation, 7, 33-34; national goals, 6, 15; outstanding issues, 17-19, 30-32, 34-36; policy statements, 23-30; price stability, 7-8, 34; scope of state enterprises, 29-30; UN seat, 3; United States relations, 3-4, 23, 87, 110; *see also* Taiwan
risk taking, 53-54, 67-68
ROC, *see* Republic of China; *see also* Taiwan

S&T (Science and Technology), 24-25, 30, 47-48, 71
Saudi Arabia, 91-92
savings, household-financing, 115; mobilization of, 16, 17, 53-54, 60-63; propensity to save, 114-16; ratio to GNP, 10, 54
Science-based Industry Park (S.I.P.), 26, 27, 41-42, 46
securities exchange, 31, 62, 64-66, 120
security, 36; of supply, 5, 15, 26
Shanghai communique, 3, 8
Singapore, competition with Taiwan, 5; Confucian ethics, 122; debt service ratio, 2; GDP growth rate, 2; GNP per capita, 2; investment in Hsinchu, 49; regional economic role, 87, 108; saving habit, 116; trade with Taiwan, 90; vocational training, 83
South Africa, 91-92
stocks and bonds, 56, 106
strategic industries, 26, 45, 53, 56, 90
structural change, 12, 14-15, 17, 24, 26, 29-30, 46, 64, 70, 90
Sun Yat-sen, 6
Sun, Y. S. (Yun-suan), 25, 27-28, 32

Taichung, 27
Taiwan, Asian Development Bank, membership in, 5; consensus-building, 33; debt service ratio, 2; defense needs, 3, 8; educational aid to Southeast Asia, 109; external condition of continuing growth, 14-15; GDP growth rate, 2; GNP per capita, 2; human capital investment and accumulation, 42-45; IMF-World Bank seat, 4, 12; indicative economic plan, 9; international economic relations, role of, 4, 12, 27, 48, 87, 94; internationalization, need for, 15; regional trade center, 108-109; student flow, 43-44; tariff reductions, 97-99; *see also* Republic of China
Taiwan Industrial Technology Research Institute, 42, 49
Taiwan Relations Act, 4
Taiwan (R.O.C.) fund, 106-07
tariff system, 98-99; *see also* foreign trade policy and customs
tax benefits, 41, 47, 63
technology, automation and computer, 26; embodied, 40, 42-45, financing transfer of,

60, 63-64, 67; level, 15; need for continuing education, 117; transfer and import of, 15, 47, 104
textile exports, 90, 92
Thailand, 15, 90
three people's principles, 6, 29
trade balance, 18, 94, 105, 111
training, fields of, 72
Trinidad and Tobago, 2
trust, companies, 30, 66; fund, 55
Tsiang Sho-chieh, 34-36
Tsinghua University, 42

Unilateral transfer, 87, 105
United Kingdom, *see* Britain
United States, disengagement, 3, 27; economic aid, 3; GDP growth rate, 2; GNP per capita, 2; investment in Hsinchu S.I.P., 49; market, 91-92; portfolio investment in Taiwan, 106-07; ROC's IMF-World Bank representation, 4, 110; Taiwan imports from, 94; trade negotiations, 97-98; *see also* Shanghai communiqué

Venture capital, 31, 67, 106
Vietnam, armistice, 3
vocational schools, 25; vocational training, 72, 76-77, 83

Wang Tso-yung, 34-36
Wei Yung, 43
West Germany, 83, 90, 92-94, 96, 109
World Bank, ROC representation, 4, 12, 110; World Development Report, 1, 2, 9
World Trade Center, 24, 27, 109

Yu-Kuo-hwa, 32

ABOUT THE AUTHOR

Born in China in 1920, Dr. Wu attended the University of Shanghai. He went to England in 1938 where he obtained his B.Sc. (Economics) in 1942 with First Class Honors at the London School of Economics and Political Science, University of London, majoring in economic theory and minoring in political science and statistics. He received his Ph.D. degree from the University of London in early 1946.

As an economic consultant and research scholar, Dr. Wu has been associated at various times with many organizations, including the former Council on Economic and Industrial Research (later CEIR), HRAF, MIT Center for International Studies, and others. He has been a consultant to the Hoover Institution on War, Revolution and Peace at Stanford University since 1960 and is also a consultant at SRI-International. He was also an External Examiner for the Department of Industrial and Business Management at Nanyang University, Singapore and for the Department of Economics at La Trobe University, Melbourne, Australia.

Dr. Wu joined the University of San Francisco in 1960 as Professor of International Business. Since 1968, he has been a Professor of Economics at the University. He is the author or co-author of many monographs and articles in addition to a number of books on the economy of Communist China, for which he is recognized internationally.

NO

DATE DUE

V 2 3 1994			

Demco, Inc. 38-293